P9-DFG-073

HALIC

By the same author

SYLA, THE MINK

HALIC

The Story of a Gray Seal

by Ewan Clarkson

Drawings by Richard Cuffari

E. P. Dutton & Co., Inc.
New York   1970

Published simultaneously in Canada by
Clarke, Irwin & Company Limited, Toronto and Vancouver

Library of Congress Catalog Card Number: 74-95465

For Bruce and Sheila

Contents

HALIC

1. The Beginning

He was born on the running tide. The sea and the rain cleaned him, the wind dried him, and the sun-hot stones warmed his body. He was an Atlantic gray seal, and his name was Halic.

Earlier in the afternoon, as the tide had begun to run north through the Sound, boiling and foaming over the ragged knives of the Half Tide rock, something had roused his mother from slumber. It might have been the change in direction of the flow of the tide, or a slight drop in the temperature of the water. Perhaps it was the urgent quickening of the life inside her that woke her and caused her to hang upright in the clear salt water, her head and shoulders exposed to the air.

It was October, and the dying breath of summer hung warm and fragrant over land and sea. To the east lay the mainland of Wales, where the crumbling cliffs slowly succumbed to the battering of the Atlantic breakers. Westward, the island of Ramsey lay sprawled in the sea like a lazy beast, its head drooped in repose, while all around, scattered like the remains of a gargantuan feast, were small islands and outcrops of rock, mere skeletons of stone, eroded by wind and salt water.

The cow seal half rolled on the surface, dived, and began to swim steadily and purposefully toward the island. She swam below the surface, her fore flippers pressed close to her sides, her body undulating with powerful strokes of her hind flippers. A shoal of mackerel, jade green and silver, flashed across her path, but she ignored them, and rising to the surface only now and again to breathe, she made her way to a small stony beach on the landward side of the island.

As she surfaced some twenty yards from the shore, her arrival was marked by another seal, who promptly surged toward her. This was the beachmaster, a bull seal ten summers old. The broad, rugged outline of his head betrayed the massive bone structure underneath, and his strong muscular neck was scarred with the wounds of many a fight.

The bull had won and claimed this beach, along with the two cows that now lay there, sunning themselves near their calves. Ceaselessly he patrolled offshore, ever ready to attack any bull that came near, even going without food lest some other male should usurp his beach in his absence. His sole interest lay in the nursing cows, and in the weeks that were to follow he would court them relentlessly, until one by one they succumbed to his wooing. Now, roaring his anger, he thrust toward the newcomer.

The cow waited, watching the broad head arrowing through the calm, sunlit water. As he drew close she struck at him, but at that precise moment he recognized her sex and swerved away, so that her white teeth scythed empty air and closed with a snap inches away from his throat. The bull promptly sheered off, leaving her to make her way to the beach. She swam toward the stones, surveying with calm eyes the occupants already couched there, and threading her way between the large boulders that lay in the shallow water. Taking advantage of the Atlantic swell, she hauled out on to the beach, and slowly dragged her body a few feet from the surge of the tide, levering herself forward on her front flippers. Then she rested, dozing as the hot sun warmed her back.

She was quite young, this being her fifth summer. Indeed, this was to be her first calf. She was in perfect condition, a land mammal who had adopted the sea as her home, needing to return to land only to give birth to her young. Her head, smaller and more rounded than that of the bull, widened gracefully to the swelling curve of her shoulders, then tapered away to her tail, and the broad, leathery blades of her hind flippers. Her eyes were large and round, twin dark orbs each surmounted by stiff curving whiskers. Her front flippers were strong and graceful, ideal for maneuvering in the water, although of little use on land. Her ears were so small as to be scarcely visible.

In the water her coat of short fine hair had a mottled appearance, showing irregular, dark gray, almost black markings, which rippled and shone against a silvery gray background. Now, as the sun dried her, her coat became a drab brown.

It was very quiet there in the afternoon sun. The other seals slept, stretched out on the stones. Only a mewing gull broke the silence. Away to the southwest lay the limitless expanse of the ocean, but it seemed that even the Atlantic slept, breathing with a steady rise and fall, while over to the northeast, the shaggy heads of Carnllidi and Penberry, towering six hundred feet above the sea, seemed shrunken and bowed beneath the blue sky.

From time to time, as the tide rose, the cow seal moved farther up the beach, rattling the stones as she heaved herself up. In the intervals she dozed the long afternoon away, shuddering at times, and shifting her position as her discomfort grew. The sun moved on, plunging the beach into deep shadow, sparkling on the wavelets that played in the Sound. A rock dove flew by, with a clap and clatter of white wings. A raven called, twice, somewhere in the high fastnesses of the cliffs, the harsh croak sounding metallic and hollow amid the silence of the rocks and sea. As the gold of the autumn gorse faded with the light, and the tide had yet an hour to run, Halic was born.

He arrived quite suddenly. One moment his mother was lying quietly on her side. Then she gave a low moan, made one convulsive heave, and it was all over. The sudden appearance of the baby seemed to startle her, for she spun round, and this act broke the short cord by which the calf was attached. Halic lay prone at the edge of the tide, and while his mother gazed at his small white form, a wavelet broke over him, drenching him with cold salt water.

Halic moaned and shifted, and his mother, who had been sniffing him nervously, shied away in alarm. He moaned again, louder this time, and began twitching convulsively, struggling to coordinate his muscles in an effort to move away from the cold, stinging spray. His mother made no effort to help him, but watched continuously, until at last he lay above the high-water mark. Here he fell asleep, exhausted by his efforts, and his mother left him, to clean herself and swim in the cool sea.

When he woke, it was night, and a full moon lit a highway across the Sound. His mother lay beside him, her warm dark bulk offering him comfort and shelter. He crawled toward her, nuzzling her flanks, and though at first she turned away, startled, she quickly welcomed him. Halic, after some inexpert fumbling, found her teats, and drank in the rich yellow milk on which he was to grow so fast. After his feed he slept again, and with the dawn came a soft, fine rain, so gentle and warm that he hardly felt it. The rain completed the work of the sea, cleansing his soft white fur of the yellow stains of his birth, so that later in the day he glowed with a pristine whiteness. The sun shone, and the wind blew kindly, and Halic took his first real look at his world.

2. Nursery Days

The beach on which Halic lay was small and steeply shelving. There was no sand, or large stretches of rock. Instead, the beach was composed of thousands of tightly packed pebbles, smoothed and rounded by the action of the waves. Towering cliffs isolated it from the land, so that approach was impossible except from the sea.

Centuries ago, the beach had been a cave, in which Halic's ancestors had lived and played, loved and brought forth their young, but the unceasing onslaught of the sea had hollowed out the cliff until at last the roof had come crashing down. The action of the sea soon cleared the debris, and carpeted the jagged chunks of rock with smaller pebbles. So the seals returned, for the lack of a roof made little difference to them. Their fortress was still impregnable.

Halic's environment was kinder than it seemed. The stones dried quickly after rain, or the fall of the tide. Their smooth roundness supported his body, and any stone which caused undue pressure soon slid away as he moved. There was no sand to irritate his eyes or skin, and every twelve hours the sea washed the beach clean.

Impressions crowded quickly into his consciousness. He was aware of the smell of wet stone, of seaweed and salt water, of the strong, musky scent of his own kind, with its undertones of oil and fish. He was aware too, of the less pleasant odor of crude oil. All the beaches were contaminated with thick dark clots of the sticky substance, and already the pelts of the other calves were stained in places, where they had lain on the oil.

He heard sounds. There was the staccato rattle of stones as one of the seals moved across the beach; the bellowing roar from an outraged parent when one of the other seals approached too near its calf; the plaintive mewing of the gulls; above all else, he heard the sound of the sea.

The music of the sea, the rhythmic repetition of a theme, with all its variations, was to be with him all his life. The surge and hiss of the Atlantic swell, the slap and gurgle of wavelets trickling through the rocks, the deep, dim, double boom as a wave thudded into a cave, compressing the air until it exploded, throwing tons of water back at the rock, these sounds, and the song of the wind, were his heritage.

Halic's dark eyes watered a little as he raised his muzzle and stared about him. Like all seals, he was born with his eyes open, and he could see well right from birth. He had no tear ducts, and when restless or disturbed the tears would roll down his cheeks so that he appeared to be weeping. Beside him, gleaming in the warm sunlight, he saw the sleek and dappled flank of his mother, as she lay sleeping. High up the beach, its rotund little body pressed tight against the cliff, lay the elder of the other two calves, sleeping soundly in the sun.

At the far end of the beach, unattended, lay the other calf, a few days older than Halic. This calf was weak and sickly, and it wailed miserably, moving its head slowly from side to side, as it waited for the return of its mother.

Above the water line driftwood lay massed on the stones, spars and planks, matchwood and broken branches, wood discarded from passing ships, washed from decks months previously as gales swept in from the southwest. Much of the wood had floated down rivers on the floods of the previous winter, and now lay, waterworn and impregnated with salt, awaiting the next stage of its journey to dissolution.

To the south and east lay the Sound, the narrow gut of water between the island and the mainland. The running tide boiled and hissed as it thrust against the mass of water, held in the Sound by a stiff northerly breeze.

Across the Sound, on the mainland coast, giant slabs of purple slate rose vertically from the sea, between domes and buttresses of wind-carved sandstone, warm and red. Weathered granite, crumbling and castellated, towered skyward, its turrets and battlements hoary with green and yellow lichens. On the clifftops, amid golden splashes of gorse, lay great purple winestains of heather. Beyond, fading into the dark and distant hills, glowed the mellow hues of the ripening land.

Halic shuffled across the stones to his mother's side. Raising himself on his fore flippers, he heaved himself forward. Then, hunching his back, he drew his hindparts toward his head. Next, thrusting down with his hind flippers, he pushed his whole body forward. Clumsily and slowly, he made his halting progress across the few yards of beach.

The clatter of his approach roused his mother from her doze, and she leaned forward toward him, their muzzles touching briefly in greeting. Then she lay back, half on her side, and in response to the caress of his muzzle on her flank her twin breasts, which normally lay flat and hidden, rose up from her short coat, and Halic began to feed.

As he sucked, she caressed him lightly with her flipper. This "flippering," a strange, rapid, almost vibrant action, performed it seemed, nervously and hesitantly, was the only gesture of affection shown by the mother for her calf. All the seals did it, especially when the calves were suckling, stopping every few moments in an absentminded way, and then hurriedly resuming the caress.

Halic finished his feed and lay still, watching the sea. The doglike head of the master bull showed briefly for a moment above the waves. A young cormorant was fishing close by, unworried by the seal, for gray seals never touched seabirds.

The cormorant was hungry. He had been fishing hard all afternoon, but because of his lack of skill and experience the fish eluded him.

Diving down, the bird thrust himself through the clear salt water, peering this way and that until he located a shoal of small fish. Then, he circled rapidly, driving the fish into a tighter shoal. Suddenly, he darted into the center of them, beak snapping wildly as he tried to capture one of the tiny silver fish.

Time and again he failed, and was forced to return to the surface to breathe. At the fifth attempt, his beak closed on quivering flesh, and he bore his catch to the surface. Although normally a silent bird, his pent up emotions found relief in a squawk of triumph, an act which almost lost him his meal, for the fish slipped from his bill and began to swim feebly away. In a second it was grabbed by the head, and swallowed.

Halic looked very wise as he lay watching. He was, in fact, a most precocious infant. By the time he was born he had already grown and shed some of his milk teeth, and had started to molt some of his baby coat, although this molt stopped when he was born. For the first few weeks of his life he was more vulnerable, more exposed to danger, and less able to protect himself, than he would ever again be. It was vital for the success of his race that this nursery period should be as short as possible.

Meanwhile, he had little to do except sleep and eat. His mother's milk was over ten times richer than cow's milk. At birth he weighed twenty-nine pounds, and from now on he would gain weight at a prodigious speed, more than three pounds each day. During this nursing period his mother would not feed herself, but draw on her reserves of fat, built up during the months of rich summer feeding. Right now she was sleek and plump, but by the time Halic was weaned, she would have lost nearly two hundred pounds, almost a third of her total body weight.

All the seals had a seemingly limitless capacity for sleep. Indeed, it seemed that sleep was their natural mode of existence, broken only by the necessity for action, stimulated by danger, hunger, or other driving force. As soon as the needs of the moment were satisfied, back they went to sleep. Now, with little fear of danger, and no desire to feed or hunt, the cow seals had little to do except feed their calves. So they passed the long days drowsing on the stones, and this helped to conserve their energy. Probably it also helped to pass the time, so that what seemed, to the human observer, to be an interminably long and dull period of confinement, was perhaps to the seals quite a brief interlude of time, unnoticed except during the brief periods of consciousness.

During this time the master bull did not feed either. He too slept for long periods, in the water or on the beach, yet he was ever on the alert for the arrival of a challenger bull, one of the many males that had reached maturity but had been unable to claim possession of a beach.

The bull was in his full vigor, for so far the strain of fasting had not begun to tell on him, and it was still too early for him to have spent his strength among the ladies of his harem. During his waking hours he patrolled to and fro in the sea just off shore, ever ready to intercept any trespasser.

Each time one of the cow seals entered the water to play and relax after a long spell on the beach, the bull would approach, but always the cow warned him off with slashing white teeth and bristling whiskers. Lazily the bull would glide away, remaining in attendance, but at a respectful distance.

A challenge came at dusk of the first day of Halic's life. The tide was almost full, and the cows lay high on the beach, guarding the calves from the impact of the small waves by sheltering the little ones with their bodies. As the uproar broke out they raised their heads inquiringly, gazing with mild interest in the direction of the noise.

The challenger bull, a lusty young male as yet unscarred by

battle, had come quietly into the Sound, following the edge of the rocks. By the time the beachmaster noted his arrival, the challenger was between him and the beach. Berserk with anger, the older bull flung himself into the attack, and, imprudently, the younger male stayed to fight.

For a moment, the sea boiled as the beachmaster reared half out of the water, striking down at the stranger whose teeth were chopping at his throat. In the nick of time, the younger bull turned his head away, narrowly avoiding death from the terrible jaws that could crush his skull like an egg. Instead the beachmaster had him by the neck, and was shaking him as a terrier shakes a rat.

Wrenching free, the young bull fled, lashing the water to white foam as he sped away, still pursued by the beachmaster. A black mist of blood hung for a brief moment where he had been. Then the sea was clear again, and the master bull returned to his station.

The cow seals drooped their heads in sleep again, and later the moon shone on the young bull as he lay sleeping on a flat rock south of the island. His wound had stopped bleeding, and the scar shone white in the moonlight.

3. Calm and Storm

The weather remained fine and calm. A few showers fell, but they were never prolonged, and as it was still early in the month the hot sun soon dried the stones. During the next few days two more cows hauled out on the beach. The first gave birth almost immediately, but the calf was stillborn. The white corpse lay neglected among the stones, until the tide took it away, south of the island, where it sank beneath the waves, to be seen no more.

The other calf, although not born until the third day after the arrival of its mother, was strong and healthy, and added its bawling to that of the others. There were now five cows and four calves on the beach, joined occasionally by the bull, and, at high tide, conditions were a little cramped. As the tide rose, mother and baby would stay in position until the last moment, until the calf was awash in the swell. Then came a general reshuffle, as the herd moved up the beach, each seal endeavoring to secure a portion of the beach for herself and her calf. This led to much vociferous argument, accompanied by aggressive posturing and a savage display of white teeth.

Very seldom did a fight develop, though occasionally a calf would get buffeted and rolled over as his mother lunged at a trespassing neighbor. Then the bleating and wailing of the injured calf would be added to the din, until at last the whole company would settle down for a brief period, only to repeat the performance as the tide rose higher.

As the tide ebbed, the seals moved back down the beach, following the receding sea. Twice in every twenty-four hours the sea crept up the beach, then fell back in response to the gravitational pull of the moon.

The sun also exerted its force on the sea, and when the sun and the moon pulled together, as at the time of the full and the new moon, the tides ebbed and flowed more strongly. These were the spring tides. The next seven days, as the planets moved in the heavens, the pull of the sun opposed that of the moon, so that the tides grew correspondingly weaker. These were the neap tides, when the pulse of the sea was least strong. Then the tides would start to grow in strength again, the sea rising higher and higher each day, and receding farther and farther down the beach.

Halic was born on the second tide after the full moon, so for a little while at least, each high tide left a little more beach exposed, thus easing the problem of overcrowding. The eldest calf was now a fortnight old, and so fat he resembled an elongated egg. His pelt was stretched as tight as a drumskin, and it seemed impossible that he could move. Yet move he did, jerking down the beach like a fat little grub, to play at low tide in the shallow water among the rugged weed-covered rocks that the ebbing tide exposed.

When Halic was a week old he too began to explore the sea. Anxiously guarded by his mother, he wriggled into the water and let the waves wash his portly little body back to the beach. As he gained strength and confidence, he began to investigate the narrow channels and pools among the rocks. He rode out to sea on a receding wave, and then, finding himself in deep water, flippered frantically shoreward, only to find himself carried there on the next wave.

Always his mother hovered nearby, ever ready to slip beneath him and support his weight if he found himself in difficulties. If the master bull came too near she would launch herself at him with the lithe speed of a leopard, and knock him sideways in the water with the fury of her attack. Meantime Halic would bumble about, practicing little dives, which invariably failed because he had not yet learned to empty his lungs of air before submerging, and because he still lacked the strength to thrust himself under. He would stand on his head, his hind flippers working furiously in the air, only to bob up again like a cork.

At this stage of his development his hind flippers were positioned palms downward, at right angles to his body. Soon they would rotate through an angle of ninety degrees, so that they would be placed palm to palm. His foreflippers were gaining in strength, and soon he would master the art of diving by pulling himself under with one sidewise stroke. Meantime he was practicing hard.

At times he explored the cracks and crannies of the rocks, nosing through the fringe of weed that hung there. He picked up pebbles and dropped them, saw and chased, but never caught, small crabs and butterfish. He found small snails—winkles, top shells, and dog whelks—and several of these cracked in his jaws as he played with them. Then he would crunch them up, savoring the strange fishy taste, and letting the water wash the shell fragments from his tongue and jaws.

When he was tired he would haul out on to the stones, bawling and grumbling until his mother came and fed him. Then, lulled by the security of her side, and bloated with rich creamy milk, he would drift into slumber, only to wake when the rising tide nudged him up the beach.

Small incidents marked the passing of the days. A school of dolphins passed, heading south down the Sound. As they surfaced their hides shone black in the sun, and the hiss of their breath came clear on the morning air.

A young raven flew in from the sea, and hurtled straight for the cliff face. At the last moment he catapulted high into the air, soaring over the island before he turned back out to sea, and repeated the performance. His arrival disturbed a pair of rock doves which were perched on a ledge below the cliff top, and they sped away, white and fluttering, into the sun, toward the mainland.

A thousand feet above the cliffs a large hawk hung stiff winged in the sky. He was a peregrine, one of the few that survived. Now he marked the doves as they climbed toward him, and he dropped from his position, speeding his plummeting dive with swift, incisive wingbeats. He hit one of the doves at the base of the neck, and it died in an explosion of white feathers. The head flew off, to drop into the sea, and the body spiraled downward toward the waves. The hawk caught it a foot above the sea and flew off with his burden.

For long periods the Sound looked empty of life. Most of the seabirds, the puffins, the shearwaters, the razorbills, and the gannets, which had been so numerous in the spring and summer, had gone, heading far out to sea to winter in the Atlantic. They had come to land only to mate and raise their young, and now the nesting sites were empty.

Some seabirds remained. The cormorants and their lesser brethren, the shags, together with the gulls and the oystercatchers, hung on throughout the year. The oystercatchers were misnamed, since they never touched oysters, feeding mainly on small molluscs, marine worms, and crustaceans.

The moon waned, and the tides rose higher. For a brief while on the night of the spring tide the whole beach was awash, and Halic, like the other calves, floated on the waves, guarded by his mother's body, until the water receded from the base of the cliff.

Of the five calves born on the beach, only three remained. The weakling calf had developed pneumonia, and refused to nurse. All day it lay at the foot of the cliff, moving little, and no longer wailing and crying. Flies came and settled on its face, and the calf brushed them away with its fore flipper.

This act transferred the discharge from its nose to its eyes, and the same organism that was destroying its lungs began to attack its eyes, making them purulent and inflamed. One night it died, and the body lay among the stones until the spring tide took it away.

The eldest calf was now three weeks old, and its mother had ceased to feed it. Too fat to care, it dozed in the sun while its mother played in the sea with the master bull. Halic, fourteen days old and seventy-nine pounds in weight, was five days older than the third calf, a female. Her mother was old, and blind in one eye, but in spite of, or perhaps because of this infirmity, she was very strong and domineering, quick to anger, and always able to secure the best corner of the beach.

Slowly, the weather was deteriorating. The wind, which had been veering north and east, and seldom blowing stronger than a stiff breeze, suddenly backed south. On the third day after the spring tide the wind was gusting strongly. By evening, storm clouds marred the fading blue of the sky, and eastward the land was dark.

Sudden squalls hit the beach, raking the stones with stinging showers of rain. The slap and lop of the waves grew louder and more threatening as the tide rose and darkness fell. The seals were restless, and their sobbing wails rose above the clamor of the waves and the roar of the wind. The youngest calf, wedged in a niche of rock on the lee side of the beach, was sheltered from the force of the wind and the impact of the breaking waves.

The eldest calf swam out to sea, away from the danger of the breaking waves, but Halic lingered on, reluctant to forsake the land for the sea. His mother called anxiously, returning to his side again and again, trying to lead him out into deeper water. Several times she almost persuaded him, and he would follow her for a few yards, but each time he turned back, to lie wailing and moaning, as the waves broke over him and crushed him against the stones.

A last the whole beach was awash, and Halic was in danger of being smashed against the foot of the cliff. Suddenly, almost without any conscious effort on his part, Halic found himself riding the backwash of a wave higher than the rest, and next moment he was clear of the beach, and out in the open sea.

Halic rose and fell in the waves, content to let the sea carry him. For a while his mother managed to keep by his side, but in the darkness she kept losing him. One moment they would be swimming side by side, and the next they would be several yards apart. Ahead of them lay The Bitches, a chain of jagged rocks that stretched out into the sound like the broken spine of a long-dead sea monster.

Here the sea boiled and thundered in a white maelstrom of foam, as millions of tons of water poured over and around the rocks. Halic felt himself carried forward with ever increasing speed, spinning and sliding as the tide carried him along. When he reached calmer water he was a hundred yards from his mother. He never saw her again.

4. The Wanderer

Dawn broke grim and gray. The wind had abated somewhat, and a steady rain flattened the waves. North of the island, and miles from the nearest land, Halic floated on the sea.

He had survived the ordeal of the storm, and, quite fortuitously, escaped the greatest danger, that of being cast up on a stormbound mainland beach, where he would have been at the mercy of marauding farm dogs and interfering humans. He had lost his mother, but he would not have fed from her much longer, and it is doubtful if he would have gained any more weight.

A thick layer of blubber insulated him from the cold, blubber that was densely interlaced with such an intricate network of blood vessels that he had fifty percent more blood than other mammals of comparable size. This thick jacket of fat would nourish him in the weeks and months to come, as, slowly, he learned the art of catching his prey.

His rich blood supply meant that he could go for long periods without breathing, and he was further aided by a sphincter muscle close to his heart that slowed down the blood supply to his extremities and reduced his heartbeat from a hundred and twenty beats a minute to less than ten. So now Halic slept on the surface of the sea. Every five minutes or so a sensation of coldness in his flippers roused him sufficiently and he raised his head above the water, eyes still tight shut, to take ten or a dozen breaths before sinking back into slumber.

Waking on the ebbing tide, he turned and began to swim with the flow. He headed south and west, so that his course took him far to the west of the island on which he had been born. He soon discovered that it was easier and more comfortable to swim below the surface of the waves, rising only to breathe now and again.

The rain had stopped, and the clouds were breaking to reveal pale sunlight and ragged patches of blue sky. The gray sea and the gloom gave way to a world of blue, an azure that deepened beneath him so that the sea bed was shrouded in mystery and shadow.

Halic was not alone in the sea. From time to time he was joined by great shoals of fish, swimming above, below and around him. Below him their jade green and blue-black markings merged with the shadows of the sea, while above their silver bellies and flanks matched the broken light that filtered from above. They were most visible from the sides, as their shimmering flanks betrayed their presence. The sight excited Halic, and he chased them as he had chased the crabs and butterfish in the rock pools. The fish easily evaded him, and sped on, but their multitudes were so vast that for long periods at a time they continued to pass him, heading southwest on the same course.

Halic came at last to the small islands that lay in the sea west of Ramsay. Here he found a small flat rock which was exposed at low tide, and he hauled out on to it to rest for a while. He woke to find darkness, and the rising tide washing the rock, lifting him from his couch and rocking him gently. A crescent moon sailed amid white scudding clouds, and the islands were dark shadows in a black and silver sea. From time to time a white light lit the scene from the lighthouse on the island known as the South Bishop.

There were other seals nearby. Halic could hear them sobbing and moaning above the hiss of the wind and waves. He swam toward them. His desire for their companionship was tempered by the recollection that, apart from his mother, none of his own kind had welcomed him in the past.

The seals were yearlings, and if they did not welcome Halic, at least they showed him no animosity. They lay on a sloping slab of rock, and Halic hauled out beside them, sleeping fitfully until dawn. Then, as the first spears of golden light shone on the sea the yearlings tumbled off the rock into the waves. Halic followed them, but he soon lost them, and found himself heading south again, across the wide mouth of the bay, toward the islands that lay in the distance.

As the sun rose above the horizon the sea ahead of him seemed to boil. Mackerel had found a shoal of tiny fish, immature cod, and were scything into their ranks, bolting them down as fast as they could catch and swallow them. A small shoal of bass, lean gray wolves of the sea, weighing six and seven pounds apiece, swam up to join them, taking mackerel and cod impartially. As Halic watched, alternately treading water and swimming closer for a better view, a triangular black fin cut the water far out to sea.

Soon there was another, and then a third, until at last there were seven, cutting through the water at terrible speed. As they reached the mackerel, the fins fell into line, encircled the shoal, and then cut in to attack. The dolphins had come to dine.

They slashed into the fish, killing and maiming, not pausing to feed. The bass fled, not stopping until they were well out of range of attack. For a while the mackerel were so engrossed in their own work of slaughter that they seemed oblivious to their danger. Suddenly, however, the whole shoal appeared to realize what was happening and, ceasing to feed, they too, sped away.

Only then did the dolphins begin to feed on the broken corpses that floated all around on the surface of the sea, chirruping and chattering excitedly to each other in their birdlike voices. Halic watched from a respectful distance. The dolphins were bigger than he, and while it was unlikely that they would have harmed him, he felt that prudence was the best policy.

In a very short while the sea was clear of the carnage, and the dolphins moved away. Halic swam into the area, moving cautiously about six feet below the surface. The sea was cloudy, and thousands of silver scales dislodged in the melee shimmered and danced in the waves. Away in the gloom, a larger flash of light attracted Halic's attention. He turned, and swam toward it. The flickering light grew brighter and clearer, and as Halic drew near he saw that it was a mackerel, still alive but swimming slowly, its spine crippled and broken by the jaws of a dolphin, but overlooked in the feast.

Halic's jaws closed round it, crushing its last vestige of life. Then he bore it in triumph to the surface, shaking it and throwing it from him so that it skittered away across the waves. As it sank, he swam after it and retrieved it, then repeated the whole performance. For some time he made no attempt to eat the mackerel, until suddenly his instinct told him exactly what to do. He bit into the fish near the neck, raised both foreflippers, and then, still holding firmly with his teeth, pushed the mackerel violently away from him.

In this manner he tore a strip of flesh from the side of the fish. He bolted this down in one piece, then swam after the corpse, seized it, and tore the remainder of the flesh from the bones. When this was eaten, he swam on, eagerly questing for more easy prey. The dolphins had done their work too well, however, and he found no more fish.

His swimming prowess was improving rapidly. As well as getting faster, he was growing more agile, for without his being aware of it, his frantic attempts to catch the mackerel that passed him had speeded up his reflexes, and taught him to turn suddenly to one side or the other. His judgment of distance was improving, and he found he was able to swim for longer periods of time without feeling exhausted.

He was beginning to lose the white coat of his babyhood,

and the mottled gray of his new pelt was beginning to show around his head and flippers.

The islands to the south were nearer now, their russet walls rising sheer from the rim of white foam that surged around the base of the cliffs. Once the islands had been highly prized for the value of the products they supplied. Seals were butchered for their hides and oil. Rabbits were trapped and sold. Seabirds were harvested, and their eggs collected at nesting time. Crops were grown, and sheep reared, but now the islands were uninhabited, left as nature reserves for the seabirds and seals to breed and live in peace.

The wind blew keen and cold from the north, churning the sea and whipping up a fine stinging spray. Halic took shelter in the lee of an island, and slept.

For the first time he slept on the seabed, sinking down into forty feet of water and slumbering undisturbed by wind or waves. When his body grew starved of oxygen, he would rise to the surface, and, still sleeping, recharge his bloodstream with the vital oxygen. Then, with a lazy wave of his flipper, he would turn and sink headfirst to the bottom.

Down there the floor was clean sand, and in the dim blue light life teemed. Flatfish, plaice, and sole, lay in dense packs, burrowing into the sand so that they lay hidden from view, or moving slowly over the seabed in search of marine worms. A dogfish, small member of the shark family, hovered nearby, ready to pounce on any flatfish that ventured too close.

Halic woke, and broke surface. The sun was setting, and the islands glittered in a golden aura of light.

Other seals played and swam in the water around him, and on a small beach two cows rested with their calves. When Halic approached, however, the master bull that patrolled the sea in front of the beach warned him away. Halic swam off, into the darkening waves, still heading south.

5. Sea Voyage

The island of Skokholm passed by in the night. Halic was alone in the open sea. What motives prompted his southward voyage can only be guessed at. He had grown accustomed, during his short life, to an area in which islands were thickly scattered, and he had no reason to suspect, if indeed he thought about it at all, that the rest of the world would be any different.

His horizons were limited, physically as well as metaphorically. He could only, at the most, raise his head a foot or so above the sea, and then often his view would be obscured by waves. His vision under water was good, but distances were dim and blurred. As yet he knew nothing of mankind, or the land beyond the cliffs.

Had he not been swept from his birthplace by the sea he might well have lingered on, long after he had been weaned, and so acquired a sense of territory. Then he might have been content to spend his life in the place of his childhood, and have seen nothing of the world. Few of his kind ever ventured far, yet he was not alone in his wandering. Other seals had traveled farther than he, some never to return. Certainly it was only through such migrations that new colonies could be formed, and fresh outposts established.

The gray seals were a proud and ancient race. Their empire ranged from the Eastern seaboard of North America and

Canada to the coast of Norway, but of the fifty thousand individuals that peopled the North Atlantic, more than thirty thousand lived on the rocky shores of Great Britain and her islands. Over two thousand of these lived off the coast of West Wales.

Great Britain was in fact the last stronghold of a species rapidly becoming rare. For centuries man has persecuted the seal, killing the adults for their flesh and oil, and raiding the breeding beaches to kill the whitecoated calves. Since the calves are helpless and small, it is more economical to destroy them with a club, rather than waste a bullet. Where there are many calves, the arms of the hunter grow tired, and his aim less sure, so it can happen that from time to time a calf is skinned before the life has left its body.

Only on remote islands, where the breeding beaches were inaccessible from land, and guarded at sea by savage riptides where no boat dare venture, could the seals survive extermination. So their numbers dwindled, until, in Great Britain at least, they were given the protection of the law. Elsewhere, their ranks are still diminishing.

On his journey southward, Halic followed a course roughly approximating the thirty fathom line. This was also the path of a current which flowed counter to the North Atlantic drift, a current formed as part of a great slow eddy caused by the main drift butting northeast into the Bristol Channel and the south coast of Wales, and slowly swirling back to the southwest. This eddy was helped by the waters of the river Severn flowing into the sea.

Whole days would pass when Halic seemed alone in a world of tumbling gray water. At other times the sea would be alive with life. Great shoals of mackerel still accompanied him. Their numbers seemed without end, yet their ranks had thinned considerably. Once they had shoaled in such vast quantities that they filled the bays and inlets of the coast, and men had scooped them out by the cartload, taking them and spreading them over the fields, plowing them in as fertilizer.

With the mackerel swam the strange, agile garfish, with its birdlike beak and its habit of leaping clear of the water. The mackerel and the gar had many enemies apart from man. Many sharks—blue shark, porbeagle, thresher, and tope—harried them on their journeying. Porpoises and dolphins thinned their numbers. They were food for any fish big enough and swift enough to catch them.

At other times Halic met shoals of squid and cuttlefish, cruising along in jerky undulating fashion, their bodies pulsating, their fins gently waving, and their arms and tentacles held neatly and stiffly before them. As they swam they changed color, now blushing dark red, then paling to pink or yellow. The color cells in their skin were elastic, and by extending the cells of one color and contracting those of another they could instantly change their hue.

Halic dived at one of the squid, thus discovering another odd trait, for the squid paled to a dead white, and released a thick black cloud of ink. The ink hung in the sea, retaining the shape and size of the squid, and a bewildered Halic snapped at it, while the squid itself disappeared into the gloom of the sea.

The wind blew unceasingly, sometimes strong and warm, gusting in from the southwest. At other times it would blow cold and clean, whistling over the sea from the north. Whenever it blew more than a stiff breeze, Halic slipped below the surface into calm water, away from the buffeting wind and stinging rain.

From time to time he saw ships; small rusty coasters with deck cargoes of timber; oil tankers, low in the water, their bows awash; and trawlers, returning to port with their harvest of fish.

The trawlers were clearly recognizable by the white gulls that hovered, wheeling and screaming, over the stern. On deck fishermen were cleaning and sorting the catch, amid a welter of fish offal, slime, and scales. When they had finished, the decks would be swilled down and the rubbish swept into the sea. Then the gulls would feed.

For thousands of years man had fished in the sea, but until the coming of the railways the numbers of fish caught had been but a tiny fraction of the supply. Then came the railways, and fresh fish could be transported to inland towns and sold there before it had time to go bad. The fishing fleets grew to meet the sudden new demand, and steam-driven trawlers replaced the old sailing vessels. As fish grew scarcer and harder to catch, the boats sailed farther and farther afield, up into the icy wastes of the North Atlantic, harvesting the sea, not only for fresh fish for human consumption, but for fish to turn into fertilizer and cattle food.

Tons of waste offal went overboard, to feed the gulls, and the gull populations grew as more food became available. If there was no fish, as when winter gales kept the fleets in port, the gulls flew inland, feeding from garbage dumps, and scavenging in the towns. They haunted the fields, following the plough, and robbing land birds, lapwings and fieldfares, of their food. They owed their lives to man's untidiness and greed.

Fish offal was not the only stuff thrown into the sea. The oceans were a dumping ground for all sorts of waste. Much of it sank, but some floated on the surface, carried by wind and tide until thrown up on to some remote beach, to litter and foul the shoreline. Halic was always investigating floating rafts of wreckage and debris, wood, bottles, old mattresses, plastic containers of all kinds, lengths of rope, and remnants of nets. The plastic was almost indestructible. Unaffected by sea or weather, too light to be broken up by the pounding of the waves, it might float around for weeks, and lie on a beach for years.

The sea held many surprises. One evening a shoal of basking sharks broke surface close to Halic, who, after one glimpse,

crash-dived and sped away. Although later he was to grow familiar with these giants, and to ignore them as harmless, his first sight of them filled him with terror.

The smallest was more than twelve feet in length, while the largest was nearer thirty. Swimming at full speed from the seabed, they leaped out of the water, rocketing into the sky to a height of twenty feet, only to fall back into the sea with a resounding splash. Their vast bodies shivered in the air, bronze in the sunset.

They were ridding themselves of sea lice, which clung to their gill arches and fins, and their behavior was unusual for what were normally slow and lethargic creatures. They had spent the summer following the plankton shoals, cruising over the face of the sea at a snail's pace, their backs showing above the water, and their great fins and tails waving in the air. Their food consisted of tiny animals, the larvae of crabs and fish, shrimps and molluscs, and this they obtained by swimming slowly along, their great shovel mouths open to dredge up their food.

As it caught on the gill plates, the food was sieved out, collected on the shark's tongue, and swallowed. Now plankton was scarce, and there would not be a fresh crop until the spring. Meantime, the gill plates of the sharks were frayed and worn with continual use. The sharks moved south, eventually to come to rest on the seabed and grow a new set of fishing nets.

The sharks' brains were very tiny, and their intellect was poor. Their size alone protected them. Only in the sea could an animal grow so large with so little effort. On land its own weight would have destroyed it, as the mass of internal organs pressed down on each other. In water the shark was virtually weightless, and so the problem did not arise. In any case, no normal legs would have supported such a bulk, and no terrestrial environment could have supplied sufficient nourishment.

One by one the sharks ceased their acrobatics, and Halic was alone once more in a twilit sea. Away to the west a light shone out over the water, and a little farther away another. By now Halic was used to lights in the sea. Ships frequently passed him in the night, their decks ablaze with white light, and their engines thrumming. Now he passed by the two lighthouses on the Isle of Lundy.

In the days that followed, winter bit into the sea. The wind grew colder, and brought stinging showers of cold rain and sleet. The surface waters cooled and sank, and thus the weather plowed the sea, churning and mixing the waters just as a farmer would plow the land. Halic romped in the waves, riding the white crests before plummeting down to the troughs thirty feet below, or diving through the wave a split second before the crest threatened to engulf him. He traveled south and west, butting into the wind, passing great rafts of seabirds riding out the storms.

Early one morning the coastguard at Trevose Head in Cornwall noticed a small seal playing in the sea, throwing a piece of cork around in the waves. The sight aroused no interest, for seals were not uncommon in those parts, and after a casual glance, the coastguard looked away. Halic continued to play with his piece of cork, riding in the surge and sway of the Atlantic swell, after being at sea continuously for more than three weeks, and journeying over a hundred miles.

6. Schooldays

Halic was now a very different seal from the one that had been washed off the beach three weeks ago. He had lost all trace of his white baby coat, and wore the mottled gray livery of a young adult. He was slimmer, for the exercise had converted much of his baby fat into muscle and sinew. He had not fed since he had caught the crippled mackerel, and he had taken nothing except a few drinks of water.

Off shore a large rock lay in thirty feet of water, and here the sea boiled and foamed as the waves broke over the crumbling granite. To landward lay an area of eddying calm, where a forest of oarweed grew, its long, thin blades waving in the tide, its stems anchored fast to the sea floor. Halic dived and prowled through the wavering brown fronds, snapping at the flickering gold ghosts of small pollack as they sped away in all directions. But the small fish proved too elusive, too protected by the jungle of weed. Soon Halic wearied of the chase and swam out to sea, where sixty feet below the waves the floor was a mixture of sand and rock.

A shoal of scallops lay quietly on the seabed, their shells partly open, their blue eyes staring in all directions. A large starfish battened on to one of their number, slowly prying open the fan-shaped shell with its five, powerful, suckered arms. The rest of the shoal panicked and swam away, fluttering through the sea like giant white butterflies as their shells opened and closed.

Halic spotted them and dived in pursuit, grabbing one and bearing it to the surface, where he crushed the thin shell and ate the flesh, dribbling out the small fragments of shell. Then he dived again, and caught two more before he lost the shoal.

Little by little, he grew more expert in hunting. His sight was keen, and he learned to prowl slowly over the seabed, watching for the faint flutter of sand that betrayed the presence of a plaice that lay buried. He caught other flatfish too, small turbot and brill, sometimes spotting them as they lay motionless, hoping their camouflage would conceal them, sometimes pouncing as they raised their flat bodies and arched their necks to take small worms and molluscs from the sand. Halic soon discovered that when fish were feeding they were often unaware of his presence until it was too late.

All the while, he drifted slowly down the coast. In turbulent weather, when the wind blew and the heaving sea was clouded with suspended silt and sand, Halic swam well out to sea, diving down through the water into the twilight of the ocean, on down until he swam in a world of deepest, darkest blue, where dark shapes moved in the shadows, and giant crabs scurried over the sea floor.

When the sun shone, and the sea was calm, he came inshore, nosing into rocky coves and inlets, swimming along underwater canyons by the side of weed-bearded cliffs, or cruising through tessellated grottoes where fishes played like birds and red anenomes clung like rubies to the stone. He came upon caves which no man knew existed, dark cavernous holes in the cliff face, just below the surface of the waves.

Sometimes when he swam into these caves they would prove to be little more than dark, water-filled hollows in the rock. From time to time, however, he found halls lit with dim green dappled light, with lofty roofs supported by giant pillars of stone. Sometimes the caves were filled with strange music, as the sea surged in, compressing the air in the cave, and forcing it out through tiny cracks and crevices in the rock face. Then, as the sea receded, air rushed back in, and it was as if someone played on a ghostly organ.

Halic liked to listen to the music as he lay on the cold, weed-covered slabs of rock. Sometimes he answered it, with moaning wails that to human ears sounded inexpressibly mournful, as if he was lamenting the death of one he loved. But to Halic, it was just a pleasant sound, comforting and entertaining. Sometimes he sang at sea, especially when the moon shone full. Then superstitious fishermen would listen and tremble, telling each other that it was the ghost of a dead seaman who had entered the body of the seal.

In the caves Halic often met other groups of seals. He joined them in hunting parties, for although the seals did not combine forces to catch fish, or share their catches, they stayed close together, and so when one found fish, the others fed too.

Together, the seals robbed the fishermen's long lines. Where the sea floor was too rough and broken for the fishermen to trawl, they set these lines to which they had attached baited hooks. The lines were left in the sea for twenty-four hours, and when the seals found them they would eat the fish hanging on the hooks.

All manner of fish were caught this way—great conger and ling, skate and ray, as well as dogfish and pollack. Those fish that were too big for the seals to tear away from the hooks they merely mutilated, biting great chunks from the living flesh. The seals had no awareness of being cruel. Fish were just food to them. Nor were the seals aware that they were robbing the fishermen of their living, but when the men found the damaged fish they cursed and swore, vowing to shoot every seal they saw.

On a bright morning in early December, Halic discovered a

strange object bobbing in the waves. Recent heavy gales had churned up the seabed for miles around, and had brought all manner of flotsam drifting round the coast.

The object Halic had found was a mine, set more than a quarter of a century ago, when Great Britain was at war with Germany. It had been overlooked when the minefields had been cleared after the war, and now, at long last, it had torn itself loose from its mooring on the seabed. Now, as Halic played with enough high explosive to sink a ship, other seals came to join him, pushing the mine around in the waves and striving to clamber on top of it.

The mine spun rapidly in the water as the seals levered with their flippers on the deadly, brittle horns. They followed it as it drifted toward the cliffs, and once two-month-old Halic succeeded in balancing on top of it, to ride for a few minutes before the mine rolled in the water and tipped him back into the waves.

At last the seals left the mine and headed back out to sea. A herring gull perched on it as it neared the cliffs, but flew away screaming as the mine lurched in the foam. For a few moments it bobbed, dark and gleaming, in the white water, and then the cliff face was torn asunder as the mine exploded. A sheep died, and two cormorants were blown to oblivion.

Far out to sea the seals panicked at the roar of the explosion, crash-diving under the waves. When Halic surfaced, he was again alone, and he swam on without seeing any of the others.

For a while, he stayed out at sea, fishing deep down, trying to catch the codling that were arriving in great shoals from the north. Before diving, Halic automatically emptied his lungs of all but a little air. This not only reduced his natural buoyancy, it also prevented nitrogen being dissolved into his bloodstream under the great pressures he had to endure. Human divers working at the same depth, and continuously breathing air, would suffer from the "bends," or caisson sick-

ness, on surfacing, because the nitrogen dissolved in their blood while they were under water would gasify, like soda water squirted from a siphon.

When, in a day or two, Halic's nerves recovered from the shock of the exploding mine, he drifted back to the coastline, to shallower waters where the flatfish were easier to catch than the swift, strong codling that had arrived for the winter.

But Halic avoided the wide flat beaches. They held little of interest for him, and he mistrusted the pounding surf and the open spaces of glaring white sand. He preferred the shelter of tall cliffs, and the surge and sway of the sea around the rocks.

In January, the sea temperature dropped still lower, and snow squalls blew in from the north and east. In the shallow waters around the coast, life was at its lowest ebb, as the fish and the conger eels, the crabs and the lobsters, moved away into deeper water, to spawn, or to shelter from the cold.

Yet the weather never stayed cold for long in that part of the world, and Halic was not affected by it in the least. Indeed, he was so well insulated that he could have withstood far lower temperatures without any discomfort.

So far he had not come into contact with mankind. Sometimes at night he had seen the lights of cottages twinkling in the darkness, but these were as meaningless and remote to Halic as the stars in the night sky. When he saw boats nearby or aircraft flying overhead, he dove deep into the sea.

7. The Estuary

One evening, as the tide flowed and the lights of a nearby town began to glow faintly in the dusk, Halic swam into the mouth of a broad estuary, questing for food. He probed farther and farther upstream as the running tide held back the freshwater flow of the river.

Life swarmed in the estuary. Ragworms burrowed in the mud and silt around rocks covered by large colonies of mussels. Tiny transparent shrimps and prawns darted through the shallow water; sand eels lay hidden in the sand. Tiny water snails clung to weed and rock, and in patches of mud the cockles, second only in number to the mussels, strained a rich diet from the ooze.

Beneath the rocks, or hiding in crevices and cracks, lived the shore crabs. They fed on anything that was meat—fish, the corpses of birds or animals, offal, their dead brethren, anything that could be torn by their pincers and conveyed to their mouths.

As Halic swam through the turbid waters of the estuary, he came upon flatfish feeding on the crabs, and his teeth clamped down across the spine of the largest, bearing the fish flapping to the surface.

Far away in the dusk, a dark shadow stirred, but made no sound. In his preoccupation with eating the flounder, Halic paid no heed to the slight movement. He dropped the skeleton

of the fish into the shallow water, where it was at once surrounded by a host of crabs, and swam off in search of fresh
victims.

The fisherman, who had been standing in the shadows at the
water's edge, watching Halic as he fed, now reeled in his line,
removed the remains of the bait that clung to his hook, and
inserted the hook in the bottom ring of his rod. Then he
picked up his bag and moved quietly away. Once clear of the
water, he walked briskly up the hill to his cottage, and putting
away his fishing tackle, he picked up a small caliber rifle and
left the house once more.

The moon was rising now, whitening the rippling water of
the estuary. The tide was beginning to ebb, and the flounders
had stopped feeding, settling down in the sand in the deepest
pools, where they remained covered with water, even at low
tide.

Halic remained in the estuary, listening. He could hear the
faint noises of traffic from the town, and the soft wind in the
trees. He heard the gurgle and splash of the water, and the
liquid plop of a rising fish. Above these sounds came others,
muffled and dim, the thud of feet on boards, a tiny metallic
clatter, the creak and splash of oars.

The sounds came from downstream, and Halic hesitated. He
was aware of impending danger, but uncertain of what form it
would take, so he hung in the water, his head a round, black
silhouette in the light of the moon. Now, very faintly, he
could make out the dark shadow of the boat, and the feeble
flicker of light as the oars stroked the water.

Then the rowing ceased, but still Halic waited, poised for
instant flight, yet curious, puzzled as to the nature of this
strange creature. Slowly the boat swung round, and all at once
the bowed back of the oarsman became a crouching, menacing
shape as the moonlight shone on a white face, and two white
hands that gripped a glittering rifle barrel.

Halic dived with the report, and the sound was welded in his mind, together with the flash of the gun and the image of the man, by the searing pain of the bullet that ripped across his neck. He passed under the boat, and away out to sea, while behind him his blood trailed like black smoke in the tide.

Never again would he enter an estuary. Never again would he trust mankind, or boats. Henceforth he would keep to the open sea, and the sanctuary of the high cliffs. Now he swam far away from the land and its dangers, and dawn was silvering the sky before he slept.

His wound, which had bled profusely for a long time, was not in fact serious. It amounted to little more than a short graze across the back of his neck, which left a white scar. The copious bleeding was due entirely to the fact that his blood supply was so very rich, and he was in no way embarrassed by the loss.

In the clean salt water the wound quickly healed, and Halic forgot about it during the next few days. He journeyed on down the coast, drifting silently over acres of mud, rock or sand.

The sea held many secrets. On the main shipping lanes, or wherever boats were at all numerous, the seabed bore unmistakable evidence of mankind. Rubbish littered the floor, some objects large and unwieldy, others small, some new and still shiny, clearly recognizable for what they were, others corroded and overgrown with marine organisms so that they were no longer identifiable.

Commonest and most indestructible of all were bottles, of all kinds, and in all shapes and sizes. Many of them had been adopted as homes by the sea creatures. A jar which had once contained face cream moved slowly and jerkily over the stones, sprouting antennae and claws. It had been appropriated by a hermit crab, instead of the more customary whelk shell.

Blennies, small fish, had discovered too that bottles were in many ways superior to shells. Normally they laid their eggs in the empty shell of a whelk, but they had discovered that a bottle with a wide neck made a far more suitable residence, and in the breeding season each jar held its precious store of eggs, while the fierce parent guarded its brood. So the manufacturers of pickles and coffee contributed to the spread of wild life.

An outboard motor lay tarnished on the sand, one of many lost by careless owners who had tried to lift them inboard without first tying them to a safety rope. Valuable equipment lay rotting and useless. Anything metal quickly corroded, eaten away by the action of the sea.

Often these areas proved to be rich feeding grounds, especially where a river flowed into the sea. Its nitrogen-rich waters were laden with crude organic sewage and fertilizers from the fields. Plant life fed on the sewage, absorbing the nitrogen and minerals. Small animals ate the plants, and fish preyed on the animals. Halic ate the fish.

The rivers carried other, grimmer burdens. Insecticides, sprayed over the land, were present in minute quantities at times of heavy rain. Shellfish absorbed these as they sieved the seawater, and the deadly chemicals accumulated in their tissues. The fish ate the shellfish and accumulated even more, storing it away in their fat. By the time Halic ate the fish the original minute trace had increased a hundredfold, to be stored in his fat. Seabirds were being poisoned in the same way, though as yet the doses were too small to be fatal. Many land birds and animals, however, along with freshwater fish, had succumbed to the poison, and for the people of the sea, it was perhaps only a question of time.

Now the days were lengthening, although the nights were often still cold. Halic came to a tiny, remote bay, cut off from the land by high beetling cliffs, where a pair of ravens had built their untidy nest of twigs, and where they now brooded their pair of young. At the edge of a small pebble beach, facing east, a narrow fissure in the granite opened up into a cave with a floor of smooth stones and flat rocks.

Offshore the stones gave way to smooth sand, rich shoaling grounds of plaice and other flatfishes. Here Halic lingered. He was now almost six months old.

8. The Black Spring

Spring had come. In the sea, as on land, the warmth and light of the sun recreated the annual miracle of life, as the tiny, jewellike plants of the plankton grew and multiplied. Soon whole areas of the sea were stained amber and emerald by these minute starlets, with glistening spikes and horns.

To feed on the plankton came hordes of tiny animals, and these in turn were cropped by shoals of small fish. Larger fishes harried these shoals, and Halic joined in the feast. Forsaking the shelter of his cave, he drifted south and west, keeping to the open sea, but never very far from land.

The day had been warm and fine, the sea rolling oily and calm beneath a saffron yellow sun. As dusk fell a smoky purple haze fell over sea and land, as dense white mist rolled in from the sea. Ahead of Halic stretched a chain of rocks, just visible above the water, the remains of what, centuries before, had been a pattern of islands. Now only the eroded skeleton of granite remained, the needle sharp peaks as jagged and numerous as shark's teeth.

Halic hung around the rocks until darkness and mist obscured every feature of the seascape. Then, as the tide turned, he hauled out on to a flattish ledge of rocks and weed. There he fell asleep. The night passed, and the ebbing tide sank lower and lower, until Halic was marooned sixteen feet above the black water. Then, just as slowly, the sea began to steal remorselessly back up the rock. Dawn came, but still the cotton wool blanket of fog blotted out all detail. Not a ripple marred the surface of the sea. Halic drowsed on, only stirring as the water lapped round him, lifting the ragged fronds of weed and chilling him with its cold embrace. As he roused himself, he was aware of a faint sound, a regular beat, muffled and shrouded by the mist, but steadily growing louder.

A ship was approaching, moving slowly and cautiously through the fog. Halic listened, and it was as if the throb of the engines echoed his thumping heart. They grew louder, nearer, until at last Halic's nerve broke and he plunged into the sea. As he swam he was conscious of a great black wall looming up through the fog, of a shrill, screaming bow wave that threatened to throw him off balance, and then the deafening beat of the ship's propellers as they cut through the sea.

At the top of the tide, the oil tanker sailed straight on to the knives of the reef, and the waiting granite ripped her hull, cutting the steel as if it were paper, until at last the ship came to a grinding, shudddering halt. Then, like a stricken whale, she lurched over on her side, and her cargo of thick black oil began to flow like lifeblood from the ragged gash in her flank.

From the stern of the ship came a tiny flowerlet of flame, an orange rosette that grew and expanded until it towered higher than the ship. For a brief moment it lit the whole scene, reddening the sea and staining the white walls of mist that shrouded the dying ship. Then the fire went out, extinguished by a giant explosion that sent a shower of debris flying far into the air. When Halic looked again the ship was alive with scurrying forms, as one by one the crew leaped overboard into the sea.

Now boats were being lowered, and one, laden with men, headed straight for Halic, who swam away through a sea littered with all manner of flotsam. Once he tried to dive, but found himself almost entangled with a massive coil of thick rope. Instantly, he surfaced again, and swam strongly toward

the distant shore. Still the boat followed him, and only when he reached the cliffs did it turn aside and head for a tiny cove. Later that day a group of excited men tried to explain in broken English how they were led to safety by a gray seal.

Back at sea, the stricken tanker lay on its side, and as the tide ebbed it settled more firmly on to the reef. All that day the oil flowed from it, spilling down the rocks and drifting slowly away on the tide. Only when the mist lifted were the watchers on the shore able to appreciate the full magnitude of the disaster. By then a savage gale began to blow from the southwest, and no salvage work was possible.

At dawn of the next day the first oil slicks appeared off the beaches, black and glinting obscenely as they floated on the swell. Within the next two days over a hundred miles of coastline were polluted and defiled.

So came the black spring, when only the gold of the gorse seemed to shout defiance to a world gone mad. Where oil pitched on the shore, life went out, totally and finally. The air reeked with the stench of coal tar and oil, and the fumes were so strong that they could be smelled over a hundred miles away. At first with stunned disbelief, and then with something akin to panic, men began to fight the oil, spraying it with strong detergent in an attempt to emulsify and sink it.

For Halic, it was the beginning of a long nightmare. The sea was crowded with boats, large and small, as the Royal Navy and the fishermen joined forces. In heavy seas, through sleepless days and nights, on decks slippery and dangerous with detergent, the men struggled to sink the oil.

On land, the hills and narrow lanes echoed to the high-pitched revving of petrol engines, as in low gear and four-wheeled drive, giant troop-carrying vehicles crawled down the steep and twisty hills, bringing soldiers and supplies of detergent. On the beaches men cursed and struggled, slipping and sliding as they fought in high winds and bitter stinging rain to manhandle the heavy drums of detergent into position. As the tide rose, bearing its filthy burden, they worked with inadequate equipment to spray the oncoming oil. At times the quantity of oil was so great that sprays had no effect, and desperately, the men poured the undissolved detergent into the running tide.

For several days Halic skulked just off shore, afraid to haul out on to the beaches, or to go too near the scene of such activity, yet equally reluctant to swim out to sea. So far he had avoided getting contaminated with the oil, but everywhere he swam he saw seabirds, their feathers clogged and matted with oil, dead or dying as they pitched and rolled in the swell. The birds had been gathering in their thousands just offshore, great rafts of puffins, shearwaters, and guillemots, prior to moving to their time-honored nesting sites on the coast.

Halic came at last to a tiny cove, its shingle beach still clean and free from oil. Here he found a cave, its entrance a mere crack in the granite face of the cliff, but inside it widened into a spacious cavern, with ledges of rock stretching far back into the darkness of the hill. At low tide the entrance to the cave was accessible from the beach, but the cove seemed remote and peaceful. Halic swam into the cave on the rising tide, and slept peacefully for the first time since the morning of the wreck.

The cove held its quota of casualties from the oil. In the crevices of the cliffs, and amongst the tumbled mass of boulders above high tide mark, seabirds crouched, unable to feed or fly, awaiting death from poisoning, starvation, or the stabbing beak of gull or crow. From time to time, as the tide rose, the curling waves as they broke on the beach brought another victim to join their ranks. A pitiable black object would pitch on the sand, struggling, trying to stand, and finally crawling away from the sea that had betrayed it.

All along the coast bands of volunteers, men, women, and children, were working to save as many of the oiled seabirds as they could. As the birds were rescued they were taken to

centers where they were bathed, in an attempt to remove the
worst of the oil, and then fed and warmed. The work was
arduous and unrewarding, since most of the victims were too
near death to save.

On the second day after Halic arrived at the cove, a small
boat came edging round the base of the cliffs. Halic, alone in
his cave, heard the throb of the engine, and then the shouts of
the crew as they landed on the beach. The rescue party, two
men and a woman, began at once to gather up those seabirds
still alive among the stones, wrapping each bird in a strip of
rag, and laying it in a basket brought for the purpose. Halic
listened as they worked along the shore, hearing their footsteps
draw steadily nearer. Now they were outside the cave, their
nailed boots crunching the gravel, and then there was silence,
as they paused at the entrance. Once more Halic heard their
voices.

The older man was speaking, voicing his thoughts out loud.
"We haven't come across any seals yet, but there must be a
few along this coast. We'd better check the cave over before
we push off."

Without speaking, the other man turned and went back to
the boat, returning with a burden of nets, rope, and several
clean sacks. He also carried a torch. Dumping his load at the
mouth of the cave he led the way in, squeezing with difficulty
through the narrow gap. The others followed, their breathing
loud and harsh within the confines of rock.

Halic lay motionless, his dark eyes watching their silhou-
ettes, and the thin pencil of light from the torch as it played
around the cave. It swept over him, blinding him, and then
passed on, only to swing back and shine unwaveringly on his
still form. The woman let out a small gasp of pity and admira-
tion. "What a beauty, and still quite young, too! What is it, a
cow or a bull?"

The older man shook his head. "Difficult to tell, but judging by the markings I would think a bull. He's quite clean. No trace of oil at the moment."

The younger man grunted, "He won't stay clean for long. There are oil slicks prowling like sharks just outside the bay, just waiting for him to come out. Besides, if any of the locals find him, they'll knock him on the head, and be only too glad of the chance. They've no great love for seals round here."

"You think we ought to take him?" queried the woman.

"Just as well," agreed the older man, "and then we can drive him across country and release him off the north coast. There's no oil up there. We can keep him in the shed overnight."

They unpacked the nets, and as the woman held the torch, the two men advanced slowly toward Halic, the net spread between them. In the wavering light they loomed huge, dark, and menacing, and the mesh of the net cast wide diamond patterns on his mottled hide.

Too late Halic sprang into action, launching himself off the ledge and moving with surprising speed toward the entrance of the cave. Next moment he was entangled in the clinging web of the net, and the weight of the two men pinned him to the floor of the cave. Still bundled in the net, he found himself thrust unceremoniously into the suffocating confines of a sack, and next moment he was hoisted into the air, and borne slowly away.

Halic was unhurt, but both men were bleeding freely, one from a gash in his leg, which had come into contact with a razor-edged rock, and the other from a badly bitten thumb. They grumbled good-naturedly as they stumbled down the beach, still flushed and triumphant with the success of their capture. The woman followed, staggering under the weight of the remainder of the gear, half proud of her menfolk, half concerned for their injuries.

After they had settled Halic in the boat, alongside the basket of oiled seabirds, she dressed their wounds, first the gash in her husband's leg, and then her son's thumb.

9. The Captives

Halic lay in the dusty darkness of the shed, conscious of a misery and discomfort such as he had never known. The wooden floor was unbearably hot to his skin, and the stifling atmosphere, redolent with strange, pungent scents, was torture to lungs accustomed to the purest of air. He dozed fitfully, shifting his position from time to time in an endeavor to find a cooler, damper spot.

Beside him were two tin baths, one holding fresh water, and the other a little seawater in which floated the corpses of several dead mackerel. The fish were stale, and Halic was no carrion eater. The water was tepid, and tainted with a thin scum of gray dust. Halic ignored both food and water.

After several hours, relief, of a sort, came when one of the men entered the shed and threw a bucket of water over him. After the shock and panic of the man's appearance, Halic felt a little cooler, but the boards soon dried, and his resting place grew as uncomfortable as before.

Time passed, and Halic slept again, to be awakened by the sound of footsteps, and the rattle of the shed door. This time both men entered, carrying a large wooden crate, which they laid on the floor, on its side. As they departed, Halic caught a faint familiar whiff of the sea, and crawling over to the box, he found it was lined with fresh weed. Gratefully, he crawled inside, and slept more easily.

When next he woke, the moon was high in the sky, its silver beams piercing the dusty windowpanes, and flooding the interior of the shed with soft light. Halic's bed was warm again, and the weed was already beginning to decompose. The smell was obnoxious to Halic, and, forgetting where he was, he lurched forward, seeking the sea.

Hunching himself across the floor, he crossed the shed until his muzzle bumped against the wall. Desperately, he moved round his prison, tearing at the boards until the nails of his flippers were red with blood. He came at last to the door, where a cooling breeze blew through a crack, and here he rested, his muzzle pressed to the gap, so that when his captors opened the door, Halic almost fell out.

The shed stood at the top of a sloping garden, and since Halic's natural instinct was to move downhill, he took off across the plot with remarkable speed. The garden was newly sown with neat lines of vegetables, carrots and spring onions, young lettuce and turnips, rows of peas and beans. Halic cut a wide swathe through the lot. Behind him, as he gained the shelter of the hedge, echoed the bedlam of the chase, as his captors ran with lights and nets, trampling underfoot what remained of the garden.

He did not get far. They came upon him as he struggled to force his way through the hedge, and bore him ignominiously back to the shed. Once more he lay on the hated wooden floor, and as the door closed behind him once again, there came the realization that he was no longer alone.

The newcomer was an old bull. His life had been rich and sensual. He liked to feel the sun warm on his hide as he lay on the rocks, and to race and dive through the breakers. Always, when he surfaced after a dive, his first lungful of air was clean and cool.

Until the clinging oil blinded, sickened, half suffocated him. Now he lay on the floor of the shed, staring into the darkness, and the harshness of his breathing cracked the silence of the night, as his tortured lungs labored to give him the oxygen he craved. From time to time he moaned.

Toward dawn he vomited a large quantity of oil and blood. His moaning ceased and his breathing grew less harsh. As the first light of day began to break his eyes closed, his great head dropped forward, and silence filled the shed.

They came and took Halic away, leaving the corpse of the old seal. Once more, despite his struggles, Halic was netted and bundled into a sack, and then laid in the back of a truck. For a long time he swayed and bounced in the sack, nauseated by the unaccustomed movement of the truck, and deafened by the roar of the engine.

At last the truck stopped, and he felt himself lifted up and carried away. All at once he began to struggle, as to his ears came the muffled boom of the surf. They laid him down on the beach, and the light blinded him as they ripped away the sack. The air was laden with salt and deliciously cool, and the sun was warm and golden.

Halic lay and looked about him. Ahead of him the green wall of the sea rushed toward him, white crested, translucent, until the wave broke and the cold spray spattered down over his face and back. Next moment he was gone. For a brief moment his head appeared, round and black above the breakers. Then he vanished again, lost in the wilderness of the sea.

Beyond flight, and a desire to rid himself of those tainted shores, he had no clear objective in mind. He swam fast and far, and whether instinct led him back, whether he followed the blueprint of recent memory, or the chart of an inherited navigational system, whatever the method, he set course straight for the island of his birth. Three days after being given his freedom, he played in the rippling waters of Ramsay Sound, the warm sun glistening on the grays and blacks of his mottled hide. He was six months old, and he was but a few ounces heavier than when he was weaned.

10. The Spring Gatherings

It was the time of the spring gatherings. Ever since February the gray seals had been arriving at the storm beaches and outlying rocks of the island, as they had done each spring since before the dawn of history. It was a time for sociability, for meeting and playing together. They spent long hours romping in the shallow waters offshore, or slept and sunbathed on the beaches and rocks.

There were no disputes over territory; none, that is, save for a certain amount of extremely noisy argument as to who should enjoy which vantage point on the beach. The seals liked to have elbowroom, and as the tide rose each individual held on to his or her station until the last possible moment, until at last the whole herd would move protestingly up the beach. Once the seals had dried out, they seemed averse to getting wet again, and yet they would idle on at the edge of the sea until the very last moment, curving their bodies away from the encroaching tide, and moaning irritably as the curling waves broke over them.

The more elderly and sedate members of the herd, who were usually also the heaviest, had their own favorite resting places, and were not above using their weight to assert their claims against any younger seal who had the impertinence to question them. Over and above such small frictions, however, all was amiability. Even the big bulls, who would have been at each others' throats in an instant during September and October, now lay side by side, or passed each other in the sea without more than a halfhearted yawn of warning.

The cow seals were in a coquettish mood. Brazenly they sought to arouse the indolent bulls, who, while not exactly fleeing from temptation, succumbed in world-weary fashion, without fire or vigor. A pair of voluptuous virgins came up on either side of a lordly bull as he swam through the green sea. They kissed his face and nibbled his neck with soft, tender bites, caressed him with their strong young bodies, slid over his flanks with sleek, tremulous movements, until he was at last roused enough to join in the dance.

Then the foam flashed with white fire as the gray curving bodies met, entwined, and broke away, until at last the bull seized one of the pair, and the sea closed over them for a few moments as they consummated their act of love.

Stimulated by the general atmosphere of excitement and activity, the adolescent seals chased each other through the surf, or carried on endless games of tag around the outcrops of rock. One found a piece of driftwood, and immediately it became a prize everyone in the gang wanted. The young seals wrestled and fought, leaping free of the water at times, so great was their excitement.

The young females taunted the males, alternately petting them and wrestling with them, rousing their ardor without permitting more than the briefest intimacy. Not all the play was sexual, yet the allure of love was always hovering near, a strange sweetness in the air that heightened the joy of living.

Shyly, Halic watched the revelers, torn between desire for companionship and fear of the larger seals. He joined a small group of calves of his own age, at one end of the beach, where they basked in the sunlight, and actively resented any threatened intimacy. The calves were easily distinguishable from the rest of the herd, partly by their small size and slenderness, and partly by the color of their pelts. As Halic's coat dried in the April sun, it paled to match the others.

During the winter Halic's livery of mottled gray had faded, so that although he still looked gray in the water, his dry coat had become a shade of pale beige. As the summer wore on, Halic would slowly shed this old coat, until by winter he would once more be sleekly gray.

The adult seals molted in the spring. Some were already sporting their new coats, while others were still shedding their old hair. Among the seals there was considerable variation in color, and although the general rule was for the bulls to have light markings on a background of darker gray, and for the females to have dark gray marks on a lighter background, this still left considerable scope for individual differences. Some of the females were marked like leopards, with small rosettes thickly patterned over a background so light in color as to be almost silver. Yet others were almost black, with markings like watered silk.

The adult cows, with their neat, rounded heads, gentle curves, and dark eyes, were as a rule easily recognizable from the battle-scarred, roman-nosed bulls, with their powerful wrinkled necks and massive, doglike jaws, yet occasionally mistakes could be made, even by the seals themselves. So it could happen that a young bachelor bull might suddenly find himself being tumbled in a most undignified manner by some absentminded old bull, before his outraged demeanor and vocal protest showed the old man the error of his ways.

Important physical changes were taking place in the bodies of the cows. They had mated in the autumn, two or three weeks after the birth of their calves, with the master bull who was guardian of their beach, but the fertilized egg, the tiny ember of life, had lain throughout the winter unnourished and dormant in the warmth and darkness of the womb.

Now perhaps the stimulus of the spring dances evoked the glandular reactions necessary for the implantation of the fertilized egg, or perhaps the glandular activity prompted the behavior. No one knows, for this is one of the mysteries of the seals' life cycle.

Certainly the social life of the seals was geared to the survival of the race. The autumn matings ensured that only the fittest and strongest bulls sired calves. The spring dances might perhaps ensure the fertility of those sowings, or they might serve to fulfill the destiny of those females who by chance had missed the autumn rites.

Occasionally a spring calf would be born, to lie fat and white among the milling throng of revelers, but whether this was a calf conceived in the autumn and grown to full term without any period of waiting, or whether it had been conceived the previous spring can not be known. The seals have their secrets, which are locked in the running tides.

On a hot night in May the mackerel arrived, their battalions surging through the Sound, ripping the surface of the sea to shreds and spouts of white foam as they tore into the drifting hordes of zoo plankton. Their striped flanks rippled as they snapped up the tiny crustaceans, darting here and there in an orgy of feeding.

They had spent the winter packed in dense shoals in hollows of the seabed, feeding but little as the ripening spawn filled their bodies. Early in spring they had gathered on the spawning beds away beyond the Scilly Isles, where the females shed their batches of eggs, up to half a million at a time, which floated away to hatch and drift with the plankton.

Now the mackerel had returned to their summer feeding grounds, and here the seals found them, tearing into the densely packed shoals and gorging until they were replete. Halic hunted the mackerel with mixed success. Sometimes the shoals were so large, and the individual fish crowded so close together, that he could not fail to catch them. At other times, the shoals were small and scattered, the fish fleeing away in all directions as he approached.

All the same, Halic gained weight rapidly as he fed on the rich, oily flesh of the mackerel. The smaller ones he swallowed whole, gulping them back with one chop of his jaws. The larger fish, those weighing more than a pound, he still had to tear apart, ripping the rich, curdy white flesh from the bones.

With the coming of the mackerel, the spring gathering gradually broke up. There was no sudden exodus from the beaches, no mass migration to the sea. The seals simply grew less social, less interested in one another, and more preoccupied with feeding. Although there were seals on the beaches all through the summer, hauled out to sleep or sunbathe, they all spent a large part of their lives away at sea, hunting and fishing, often for days at a time.

From now until the autumn they would build up the reserves of blubber which would support and nourish them through the long fast of the breeding season. The cow had to nourish the growing calf within her body, and store up reserve supplies of nourishment in order to be able to produce the rich milk needed when the calf was born. Finally, the cow had to be strong enough, after giving birth and nursing her calf, to face the cold and hardships of the winter.

The bulls too needed to build up their strength for the breeding season, when they would expend their energies mating and fighting for possession of the breeding beaches. So throughout the summer the seals ate and slept, reaping the rich harvest of the sea.

For the younger seals, life in the summer was not quite so earnest. Groups of young adolescents played around the rocks, and on still nights their voices could be heard, raised in sobbing chorus above the lap of the waves. But Halic remained solitary and unattached. Like the other seals of his age group, he seemed reluctant to engage in any familiarity, and often, as other seals frolicked together close by, he could be seen alone in the water by the rocks, playing with a strip of weed or a piece of cork, apparently content and self-possessed.

11. First Summer

Throughout the long sunny days and warm nights the sea teemed with life, and for days at a time Halic deserted his beach and went exploring.

He swam far out to sea, until the island was a hazy blur in the distance, and the dark and brooding hills of Wales melted into the sky. Here he found a rich hunting ground, where the submarine spine of a chain of rocks rose thirty feet from the seabed, causing the racing tide to boil and foam in a turbulent overfall where no boat dared to venture.

Here he played and fished, riding the wild waves and diving down to hunt the pollack that hung golden and shimmering above the dark and jagged rocks. The fish were of all sizes, from a few ounces in weight to giants of ten or fifteen pounds apiece.

Halic caught a number of pollack, all around two or three pounds in weight, but although he tried often enough to capture the larger fish, they were always too fleet for him. As he dived on them they shot away, melting into the jungle of weeds, and the shock wave of their sudden departure slapped him in the face.

Halic was able to stay out on the reef for long periods because, like all his kind, he drank little. Occasionally he took a mouthful of seawater, and sometimes, when he came upon the mouth of a stream, or a waterfall cascading down the cliff into the sea, he would drink the fresh water as it fell. But in the main, he got all the moisture he needed from the fish he ate. Their body fluids were much less salty than the sea.

What little fluid Halic lost was soon replaced, for the fish he ate were fresh and juicy, their flesh quite unlike that of fish which have been caught and kept out of their environment, even for a short length of time.

Pollack were not the only fish that inhabited the reef. A remarkably thin fish, shaped like a plate, with one large black blob on its gray flank, hovered near the precipitous edge of the rock. From the front it was almost invisible, and it waited in ambush for some small, unsuspecting fish to swim nearby. Then the John Dory, its black blob flickering and paling with excitement, suddenly shot its telescopic mouth forward, and the little fish was engulfed before it was even aware of the danger.

Halic ignored the John Dory, and swam downward, rolling over and swimming on his back, scanning the seabed with his keen eyes. At his approach a large skate rose from the gravel, and began to swim upward through the water, flapping along like some great brown bird. Halic darted in pursuit, and the skate, feeling the vibrations of his approach, accelerated, moving away with surprising speed.

Halic surged forward, and his jaws closed round the flapping wing of the skate, which tore itself away. Halic closed again, this time gaining a more secure grip, and the skate, which weighed close on thirty pounds, fought wildly, dragging Halic along in its efforts to escape. Its long, whiplike tail came sweeping across, lashing Halic's neck and chest, but he hung grimly on, his eyes closed, stoically enduring the buffeting and the stinging cuts of the tail.

Slowly the skate weakened, and Halic bore it in triumph to the surface, where he tore great lumps from the living flesh, allowing the skate to flap feebly away as he bolted his meal. Time and again he plunged after it and caught it as it sank

through the water, until at last little remained but the head and backbone. By now Halic was so bloated that he could barely swallow another mouthful. He let the carcass drift away down into the sea, and slept in the waves. It was thirty-six hours before he recovered sufficiently to go hunting again.

Many of the inhabitants of the rock lay hidden for most of the time. These were the conger eels, which lived in cracks and crevices among the rock. Occasionally one would emerge, its long gray body undulating and quivering, as it prowled away in search of food. One of the eels was a giant, more than three times as long as Halic, and as thick around.

The first time Halic saw the eel was when he went to investigate a violent struggle taking place near the rock. An octopus was fighting with a lobster, struggling to overpower it with its eight suckered arms. Barely had it succeeded, and was settling down to its meal, when Halic saw the great form of the eel glide toward the octopus.

The octopus saw the eel and, paling, it released a cloud of ink and shot off toward the rock. The conger surged forward and grabbed the octopus, which promptly wrapped its arms about the head of the eel. It was all to no avail. The conger simply threaded its tail through a coil of its body, thus tying a half hitch in itself, and slipped through the knot, brushing the octopus off. Next moment it had seized its prey by the head, and the arms of the octopus hung limp.

Halic kept a respectful distance. He was too small to attempt to deal with the conger, and indeed he might well have come off second best in the tussle. The jaws of the eel were strong enough to sever one of his flippers, and any struggle with the monster would have been so prolonged that Halic would have drowned long before he had killed the eel. Although he saw the conger on several occasions after that, Halic never molested the eel, and the conger never showed any interest in him.

Halic was lying on the surface of the sea, when his attention was caught by the behavior of a flock of terns, diving into the sea, quarreling and screaming. Past experience had taught Halic that this meant fish, probably mackerel, which would also be harrying the shoal of fry on which the seabirds fed.

He swam over, diving below the surface as he approached the commotion. There were no mackerel present, and as Halic drew near, the fish, in an endeavor to escape from the terns, formed themselves into a pod, a compact ball of living fish, which began to sink slowly through the waves.

Seeing the great shimmering orb slowly disappearing, Halic dived at it, and to his surprise passed right through, to emerge glittering with tiny scales which had rubbed off the fish. Turning, he tried again, and once more felt the globe part, as he slid through thousands of quivering bodies. On the third occasion the pod split up and became a shoal of little fish again, much to Halic's disappointment.

But Halic soon discovered where he could find an easy meal. In a narrow submarine ravine, stretched by the tide between two sheer walls of rock, hung a fishing net. It might have caught on some obstruction while it was being used, and broke away from the fishing boat. It might have been washed off deck, or swept away from some beach on a high tide, to drift in the sea until it came to rest against the rocks.

Now it was set permanently, for marine organisms had cemented it firmly to the rock, and being made of nylon it was virtually indestructible. Unless some gale tore it from its moorings, it was there to catch fish for all time, night and day, summer and winter, without anyone to harvest the catch.

Except, of course, the creatures of the sea. Tope and conger took each captive almost before it had finished struggling, and though occasionally a corpse would hang for a while, undulating in the ripple of the tide, sooner or later some prowler or another would find and take it. Halic visited the spot regularly, once unwittingly acting as a marine sheepdog, and driving a panic-stricken flock of mackerel into the waiting meshes.

Although this was the only ghost net Halic ever found, their number was increasing all round the coast, as fishermen forsook the old nets of twine, which rotted so quickly and which had to be continually preserved with creosote, in favor of the newer, lighter nylon nets, which would not rot. Each drift net or trawl that was lost went on fishing, year in and year out.

There was no set pattern to Halic's day. He hunted when he was hungry, and slept when he was full fed, lolling on the waves, hanging bolt upright in the water with just his muzzle showing above the sea. Or he would sink headfirst to the seabed, to lie inert among the waving blades of kelp, rocked by the faint action of the sea.

For several days he hung about the reef, and then quite suddenly he departed, swimming through the sea at a steady six miles an hour, until he reached the island. Here he hauled out and fell asleep as though he had never been away.

Each time he returned to the island he was a little sleeker, a little heavier, and his coat shone paler as the sun dried it. Life at sea was richer and far more rewarding than it was close inshore. Food was more plentiful, and easier to obtain. Except for the fact that half their number were usually away at sea, so large a colony of seals could not have existed on the island.

12. The Killers

During the first few months of his life Halic often went without food, sometimes for long periods at a time. He was still learning the art of hunting his prey, and at times his lack of skill forced him to take the food most readily available. He ate scallops and mussels, shrimps and prawns, any small creatures whose movements or scent attracted him. Some creatures, such as the starfish, he rejected after the first sampling.

Gradually, he settled on a diet of fish, which he ate to the exclusion of all other creatures, except for squid, cuttle, and octopus. When these were available Halic, like most seals, preferred them to fish.

Among the scattered boulders around the island, exposed by the falling tide, lay several rock pools, miniature lagoons formed by depressions or hollows in the rock. Weeds, brown and green, clung to the rocks, where anenomes spread their pale fronds to trap the zooplankton. Crabs and prawns hid behind the fringed curtain of the weed, and small blennies and butterfish darted to and fro.

Here, when the sun was hot, the seals loved to come to splash and wallow, or to sleep in the warm sunlit water. Here, on a dark moonless night, the ebbing tide deposited a grim burden.

At dawn, Halic found the headless corpse of a half-grown seal in the shallow water. He approached it warily and sniffed, shying away in alarm. Other seals examined it. Each took one brief look, then turned away. It was beyond their comprehension, but in a vague way it was offensive to them, and disturbed them enough so that they left it alone.

The next tide took it away, and the seals forgot about the incident. They slept, played, and departed for prolonged fishing expeditions. Some did not return, but this was not unusual, and there was no one to keep a check on arrivals and departures, or to mourn the loss of a relative.

Yet something was wrong. From time to time seals would swim in from the sea, exhausted and blowing, their flanks heaving with the exertion and their eyes filled with terror. Even the mature bulls were not immune, and this unease imparted itself to the entire colony, so that the seals grew more nervous, more inclined to panic at the slightest warning.

The frightened seals which had returned from the sea were now reluctant to leave the beach, and when hunger forced them out, they swam warily and cautiously, hugging the high cliffs. As soon as they were full fed they returned, hauling out high on the beach, away from the tide.

One day an old bull swam slowly and wearily in from the sea. For some time he lay in the water at the tide's edge, from time to time making an effort to haul out. Each time he failed, seemingly too clumsy or weak to make the necessary effort. When at last he succeeded, the reason was plain. His left fore flipper was missing completely, and a great wound ran from his jaw down his neck, extending down his flank.

Flies gathered on the wound, which became matted and festered. For a few days the bull lived on, but gradually his strength ebbed. He had lost too much blood, and with every slight movement his wound broke open and started bleeding afresh. His breathing grew shallower, his pulse more feeble and rapid, until finally his heart fluttered and stopped. He lay with his eyes wide open, staring out over the sea as though waiting for it to come and claim him. Next morning his corpse had gone.

Halic swam far out in the bay, with ninety feet of water between him and the sand, and a fresh wind whipping the wave caps. He had fed well, and was drowsy and lethargic. Suddenly he was jolted awake by the violent hiss of indrawn breath, louder and more terrifying than anything he had ever heard.

For a brief moment he gazed at the tossing green wilderness surrounding him. Then, at the sight of three tall black triangular fins, slicing through the water toward him, he crash-dived. As he turned, he caught a glimpse of a gigantic black shape, irregularly marked with dirty white. He saw the great jaws, armed with vicious teeth, and small glittering eyes.

The killer whales had moved down from the Arctic, killing and maiming as they traveled, a bloodthirsty trio for whom no prey was too large or fierce. They were the most accomplished assassins of the sea, combining great strength and speed with a voracious appetite and a grim intelligence. The big male was almost thirty feet in length, and his dorsal fin towered a full seven feet above the waves. The females were half his size, but still formidable in speed and strength. They roamed the seas of the world, from Greenland to the Antarctic, and they killed whether they were hungry or not, harrying porpoise and seal, and banding together in packs of up to sixty or more to rip the living flesh from the great whales.

In his first dive Halic had turned seaward, but within a few moments the killers were gaining on him. A split second before the male struck, Halic turned and shot off back toward the shore, skimming so close to the seabed that he raised flurries of white sand.

He had gained some distance. The killer whales lacked his ability to turn so swiftly, and had traveled many yards before turning in pursuit. Now they were gaining on him once more, and Halic darted away at a tangent as the male struck again, gouging into the seabed with a force that plowed a great furrow in the sand.

Now Halic doubled back again, passing so close to one of the females that her teeth grazed his flipper, drawing a thin dark line of blood through the water. Halic longed to surface, to draw breath into his tortured lungs. His heart was hammering, his pulse pounding in his head, and his body was growing stiff and strangely heavy to move. He felt he was moving more and more slowly, as his oxygen-starved muscles reluctantly obeyed the demands of his will.

Yet he knew instinctively that once he left the safety of the seabed, he was doomed. Once he surfaced to breathe, once he gave the killers the chance to encircle him, they would destroy him. So he fled on, twisting and turning, evading his pursuers time and time again, all the while desperately seeking some sort of shelter, a rock, a cliff face, even a dense jungle of weed.

They were gaining on him again. He was actually buffeted by a great tail as he twisted to the left. Suddenly he was aware that he was almost beaten. Fear clouded his mind. Every fiber of his body ached with fatigue, and his heart hammered painfully against his rib cage.

Quite suddenly he was alone. Dimly he was aware that the sea had grown lighter, that the sandy bed was shelving steeply upward, and that he was being rocked by the motion of the waves. As he surfaced lights flashed in front of his eyes, as air flooded his lungs and he hung, gasping and blowing, in an agony of relief. With consciousness, fresh fear returned, and he looked frantically around for his pursuers.

He saw them a hundred yards away, patrolling to and fro through the waves. The shallow water of the bay had proved his salvation, for the killers knew that if they dared to follow him, they could find themselves stranded on the beach. Now they waited, for the moment cheated of their prey, yet ready to attack again the moment Halic left his sanctuary.

For a while Halic watched them, but at last, satisfied that he was no longer in any danger, he drifted off to sleep, rocked by the motions of the waves, and carried shoreward by the Atlantic surf. Every so often he would awake and swim back out to sea, but always the menacing fins hung offshore, ever alert and ready to renew the attack.

During the afternoon Halic began to edge southward across the bay, still hugging the shore and not daring to venture out into deep water. Rain clouds were gathering, and the wind was freshening from the north, breaking the steady rhythm of the surf and imparting an uncomfortable lop to the water. Weary and ill with his exertions, and unable to dive into deep water, Halic began to feel seasick, and his nausea added to his general misery. Behind him lay the beach, with its wide expanse of glistening white sand, and its population of herring gulls and oystercatchers.

Yet Halic was reluctant to haul out on this particular beach, for it was not protected by cliffs or isolated in any way. Beyond the beach lay a road, and from time to time traffic roared past, tiny toy metallic shapes which unnerved him with their noise and movement. He was almost tempted to make a run for safety out in the ocean.

The porpoises saved him. They came swooping into the bay, cutting up a shoal of mackerel, and so fast were they traveling that they were within range of the killers before they suspected anything. At the last moment, as they realized their danger and turned to flee, the killers surged among them, their great black bodies rising above the waves as they attacked, and within moments the sea was boiling with the struggles of the doomed beasts.

One porpoise wallowed helpless in the waves, its tail flukes severed by one mighty chop of a killer's jaws. Another floated dead, its head torn and macerated, with gaping wounds on its neck and flanks. Yet another was completely dismembered. Deep in the sea the killers were wolfing down the remains, filling their capacious stomachs on the hot raw flesh. In a very short while, so voracious were their appetites, there would be nothing left of the three victims. The remainder of the porpoise school had fled, and soon the killers departed, leaving behind no trace of their work, save streaks of red on the foam-capped waves.

Alone in a gray and empty sea, Halic swam cautiously down the coastline, away from the island, and the sunlit waters of the Sound. His whole body cried out for rest, for the uneasy slumber of the afternoon had done little to repair the damage of his ordeal, and the nervous tension of the waiting had exhausted him still more.

Darkness came early, as the wind increased in force, driving ragged black clouds low over the surface of the troubled sea. Rain fell, sharp and stinging, blowing in fierce squalls that rattled like hailstones on the waves. Halic turned and swam out to sea, until the beach and the flower-strewn cliffs were lost in the gray of impending night. Overhead seabirds wailed as they sailed storm tossed through the sky, blown like scraps of white paper into the thickly gathering dusk.

At last, far out to sea, Halic slept, and throughout that wild night, and all through the following day, as the summer gale spent its short, savage fury, he lay as if dead, rising to the surface only to breathe, not once opening his eyes or caring where he was. During that time the tide ebbed and flowed twice, and on the ebbing tide, backed by the howling wind, he drifted south at a rate of six knots.

He woke fresh, all stiffness gone, and ravenously hungry. The gale had blown itself out and the sun sparkled on a heaving, tumultuous sea. The air was clean and cold and fresh and the sky was bright with yellow light. Halic took one last look around and dived, hunting for food.

There was nothing. Halic swam on until his lungs were almost bursting, and then surfaced. All round him stretched the seemingly limitless expanse of the sea. There was no land in sight—no rocks, no coastline, not even a boat. Halic breathed out and dived again.

He went down and down, into the deep violet light of the sea, deeper than he had ever gone before. At two hundred feet he turned, and swam back to the surface. The ocean seemed bottomless. Now he swam on, and suddenly, ahead of him, he saw the familiar boil of a shoal of mackerel. He surged after them, and soon he savored the richness of firm, juicy white flesh.

13. Seascape

Far out at sea a dumpy little black and white bird floated on the oily swell. Each time it was lifted to the crest of a wave it would rise from the water and flutter northward on short, rapidly whirring wings, only to pitch in the trough of the wave and wait for the next lift. The bird was a little auk, or dovekie, and the gale had blown it far from its feeding grounds away to the north.

Now, slowly but steadily, it was making its way back. It had plenty of time, and since it spent the greater part of its life riding the waves, it was more at home on the sea than on the land. When necessary it could fast for long periods. Now it fed as it traveled, diving down into the green world below the waves and hunting small crustaceans and tiny fish, on wings as well adapted to swimming as they were for flying.

The only time that the dovekie was in any danger was when the wind blew strongly toward the land for any length of time. Then the little bird might find itself carried away from the sanctuary of the deep sea, to be cast up on some storm-bound beach, or worse, be swept inland, where it would die.

The little auk was one of many species of birds that had forsaken the land for the sea, returning, like the seals, to remote and inaccessible shores and islands, and then only to breed and raise their young. Such a way of life had once proved so successful that although they were slow to breed, and produced but one youngster at a time, their populations were so vast that at breeding time their hosts thronged the cliffs and rocks from the Faroes to Brittany, and rafts of feeding birds darkened the surface of the sea.

For centuries their chief enemy had been man. At first his numbers had been few, and he took adult birds and eggs from those breeding stations most accessible to him. The birds on the remoter islands and cliffs were spared, and the predations of mankind seemed to make little difference to their numbers. Indeed, the population as a whole perhaps benefited, by being relieved of the evils and dangers of overcrowding. To the tough, self-sufficient islanders of those times, the seabirds represented an important aspect of survival in a life that was often harsh and grim. They were an annual crop, the success or failure of which might mean the difference between existence or death from starvation during the short dark days of winter.

There came a time when man's ability as an explorer exceeded his skill at being able to foresee, and for one seabird, at least, this meant extinction. As fishing fleets increased, and world trade grew, the number of sailing vessels multiplied. The ships carried large crews, and were often ill provisioned, so that it became the custom to call at the breeding places of seabirds, raiding the nests and killing off the brooding birds to supplement the ship's rations with fresh eggs and meat.

One bird in particular was singled out as a victim in these raids. The great auk was large, standing almost three feet high, and its carcass provided more than one meal for a hungry man. Its egg was correspondingly large, and these were collected by the bucketful. Moreover, the great auk was flightless, and so powerless to escape the marauders who came from the sea. By the year 1850 there were no great auks left alive in the world.

The other seabirds, the guillemots and razorbills, the puffins, the shearwaters, the petrels, gannets, kittiwakes, and terns, managed to survive, although frequently in fewer numbers.

Now a new and more insidious menace threatened them, for with the coming of the internal combustion engine, mankind needed vast quantities of oil. The thick black tarry sludge was transported in specially designed ships, and it was the habit of the ship's master, after discharging his cargo, to wash the residue of the oil from the holds, discharging the sludge into the sea.

Beaches all over the world were becoming fouled by great clods of black tar, and although legislation was introduced making it an offense for a tanker to clean its bilges at sea, it was impossible to enforce the law. Tanker captains continued the practice, and those that were caught were treated so leniently that the punishment acted as no deterrent to the others. Meanwhile, their feathers clogged and matted with the oil, seabirds were dying by the thousands.

Many of the cliffs and islands where the birds bred had been declared bird sanctuaries, and the birds and their eggs protected by law. For most of their lives, however, the birds were out at sea, and even when they were nesting they returned to the ocean to catch fish for their young. For much of the time they were totally unprotected.

The majority of the oil slicks were comparatively small, and in time they broke up, gradually decomposing. The birds which were affected most were the guillemots, razorbills, and puffins, which swam under water to catch fish, and which were prone to surface under an oil slick. Indeed, sometimes it seemed that the oil held an almost magnetic attraction for these birds, perhaps creating an illusion of calm water.

Halic saw corpses floating on the surface of the sea. On many beaches the red raw bones of a seabird, scattered and broken among the stones, bore mute testimony to the death toll. Slowly but surely, these birds were going the way of the great auk, which became extinct before man had thought to learn something of its way of life. The breed now rests among the anonymous dead of this world, and most of mankind has yet to learn to mourn its passing.

The little auk was soon out of sight amongst the waves, and Halic was once again alone in the endless wilderness of the sea. For days on end Halic's solitude was complete. Most of the seabirds were on the coasts, raising their young. He saw few boats, and even the fish were sporadic in their appearance, sometimes occurring in vast shoals, while at other times they would be completely absent.

Over all lay a peace and silence totally unknown on land or by the coast. No waves broke, or crashed with slow, ponderous force against rock or cliff. Only when the wind blew was the silence broken by a faint hiss, and on calm days the snort of expelled air, as Halic surfaced after a dive, sounded preternaturally loud.

Beneath the waves it was quieter still, a dim green world where shadows grew and faded, where shapes were faintly seen, and then only for a brief instant. Halic swam deep down, his ears and nostrils firmly closed against the salt water, the twin pads of gristle below his nostrils quivering, each pad sparsely covered with stiff whiskers.

Halic used these pads to help him locate his prey, especially when it was dark, or the water clouded or deep. It was as if he owned his own private radar screen or echo sounder. Whatever the mechanism was, it functioned very efficiently, and by this means many gray seals who were totally blind could hunt and catch fish just as easily as those who could see. Halic was probably aware of the presence of his prey before he had even seen it, and could be moving in to kill before the victim was alert to the attack. Certainly he was alive to every small movement, probably by means of vibrations transmitted to his muzzle through the sea.

Once again he had forsaken the land, and now drifted on the open sea, without any fixed goal or objective. It may be that his narrow escape from death at the jaws of the killer whales had left him uneasy about the safety of that particular coastline, and had effectively overruled any desire to return. In fact, the appearance of the killers had been most unusual, and never again in his life would he meet with their kind.

The sea was warmer here, and for days at a time the sun blazed down from a cloudless sky. The wind was set fair from the south, bringing currents of water from the Mediterranean and the coast of Africa.

Halic had now journeyed farther than ever before. His course had taken him far out into the Atlantic, passing far to the west of Land's End and the Scilly Isles, into the Bay of Biscay. Ahead of him now stretched a rocky coastline, very similar to that of Cornwall, with high cliffs, sandy bays and small wooded estuaries. Beyond this, fading into the blue haze of evening, lay the mountains of Spain.

14. The Coffers of the Sea

In the months that followed Halic drifted slowly eastward along the north coast of Spain, from Corunna to Santander. Here the light was stronger than on his native coasts, and the sea illuminated to far greater depths. Here for the first time Halic found shoals of tuna, the rovers of the Atlantic.

The tuna were like large, deep-bodied mackerel, and were, in fact, closely related. They lived long, and grew to a great size, some of them weighing over a thousand pounds. They could swim for long distances at speeds of up to nine miles an hour, and they never stopped swimming. By the time they were fifteen years old, some of them had swum over a million miles, inscribing a great arc in the ocean, across to America and then northeast to Britain.

Most of the tuna Halic saw were small, each fish in the shoal approximating three pounds. They made excellent eating, and Halic gained weight fast on the rich fare. The Spanish fishermen also hunted the tuna, catching them on lines armed with brightly colored feather lures. Sometimes when the fishing was good their boats would be so loaded that they were dangerously low in the water, and threatened to founder in the Atlantic swell.

The tuna fed on sardines, small silvery fish that glittered by the millions in the warm sunlit seas. Fishermen harvested these too, each year taking thousands of tons. For the Portuguese, farther south, the little fish represented almost half the total weight of fish caught. Still they seemed to survive the onslaught, and to carpet the sea with their numbers.

One morning a whale surfaced close to Halic, bringing back vivid and uncomfortable memories of the killer whales, and causing him to start nervously. Although the whale was of uncertain temperament, and liable to capsize a small boat that approached too near, it was quite harmless if unmolested. It was a humpback, about fifty feet long, with a short, deep body, and a large hump, which gave it its name, beneath its dorsal fin. It had large tail flukes, and its front flippers were over twelve feet long. In addition, the leading edges of its flippers were covered with large tubercles, and among the tubercles a prolific growth of barnacles occurred, giving the whale a somewhat untidy appearance.

As the whale surfaced it blew, sending twin jets of what looked like condensing water vapor into the air. In fact, the atmosphere was too warm for condensation to take place, and the fine spray was caused by a mixture of air and a fatty emulsion.

When the whale dived the air remaining in its lungs was compressed by the pressure of the seawater, and forced from the lungs into rigid sinuses which continually manufactured a fatty secretion. This emulsion absorbed the nitrogen gas in the air, which would otherwise be dissolved in the bloodstream under pressure. The nitrogen-charged emulsion was then discharged when the whale surfaced.

Since dawn the whale had been feeding on sardines, swimming slowly through the shoals of small fish with its mouth open, so that the sardines were trapped against the fringed arches of baleen plates that ridged the roof of its mouth. From time to time the whale would clear the arches with its tongue, until it had consumed about a ton of fish and was comfortably full.

Now it rolled about on the surface of the sea, its ragged

black flippers waving ludicrously, and its tail flukes slapping the water with a report like a cannon shot. This Croesus of the sea was so rich that it could afford to indulge in a ton of sardines each morning for breakfast. Yet compared with other whales it was quite a small one.

Gradually the whale's frolics ceased, and for a moment it lay quietly in the waves. Then, slowly, like a ship that has been holed in the stern, it sank quietly beneath the sea. There was a mighty swirl in the water, and the whale was gone.

Reassured, Halic swam on, journeying slowly over the sea-bed, his hind flippers waving from side to side, and his fore flippers hanging down, acting as stabilizers and keeping him on an even keel. When he had to move fast, these fore flippers pressed close to his sides, to cut down water resistance.

Many times, as Halic explored the seabed that lay off this wild and rocky coast, he passed over ancient wrecks, ships which had sunk centuries before and which now lay rotting in the ooze. Many of the wrecks held treasure. There were Spanish galleons laden with their plunder of gold, silver, and precious stones, which had made the long, arduous sea voyage from the Indies, only to founder within sight of home. Phoenician traders with cargoes of copper, tin, and lead ore from the shores of Britain; Greek and Roman vessels; pirate ships and men-of-war—all lay at the bottom of the sea, many uncharted and unknown to mankind.

The more perishable cargoes had long since vanished with the timbers of the ship, but the stones and metals remained, often scattered over a wide area of the sea bed. To Halic, this wealth was of less importance than the fact that these wrecks were often the haunts of fish and conger eels. Octopuses especially liked to hide in the caves and crannies provided by the wrecks, and for Halic, these cephalopods were a favorite food.

The surface of the sea was littered by more recent wreckage, objects large and small, drifting at the mercy of wind and tide. On an afternoon in late summer, when the sea lay flat and oily under a clear sky, Halic spotted a strange dark shape that wallowed on the surface of the sea, a shape that moved from time to time, in a curious, jerky fashion.

Puzzled, and intensely curious, Halic swam closer. The object was a dead horse, a pony that had been one of a cargo of live animals that were being shipped from England to the continent. The crossing had been rough, and the pony had died of seasickness, to be thrown overboard and left for the garbage collectors of the sea. Now the scavengers were busy at their grim work, and the corpse of the pony bobbed and swayed in the sea as a pack of sharks worried and tore at the flesh.

Too late Halic realized the danger. The sharks were all around him, hovering silent and menacing, watching him with cold eyes. Halic swam slowly and warily, anxious to avoid any sudden movement that might provoke the sharks into attack. Most of them were small, and those that hovered in the sea around the corpse were full fed and lethargic. Others still tore at the carcass. They could not bite off a mouthful of flesh, and so swam at full speed toward their prey, sinking their teeth into it, and relying on the force of their attack to tear away a portion of food. As long as they remained preoccupied with their feeding, Halic was safe from attack.

Halic was almost clear, when a small blue shark detached itself from the ring and swam toward him. Halic increased his speed slightly, but the shark followed, gaining on him until Halic could see the rows of irregular, sharp white teeth in the wide gash of the shark's open mouth. He slowed down, waiting until the shark was underneath him and cutting up to attack. Halic stopped dead in the water, and with lightning speed he dived on the shark, catching it at the back of the neck and biting with all the force of his terrible jaws, deep into the backbone of the fish.

The shark pulled free, and Halic fled, determined to put as

much distance between himself and the killers as he possibly could. Behind him the shark flapped wildly in the water. It was not dead, but its movements were uncoordinated, and its tail flapped to and fro, swinging in ever widening arcs until, incongruously, the shark caught its own tail in its jaws and held on tight, spinning like a great wheel through the sea.

A thin mist of blood drifted down to the other sharks, leading them to the cripple. Within seconds the blue shark had vanished, torn to pieces by the rest of the pack.

Halic was by now well clear of danger, but still he sped on, fleeing over the seabed until the water grew shallow and sunlit, and he could see his own shadow black against the sand. He surfaced to find himself off a small, gravelly cove, surrounded on all sides by cliffs thickly clad with heather and juniper, towering up into the sky. For a time he watched and listened, but nothing disturbed the silence save the mewing of a lone buzzard, circling somewhere above the cliffs. Satisfied all was well, Halic hauled out and fell asleep on the stones.

When he woke it was dark, and a hot, gusty wind was blowing, rustling through the heather and sending small twigs tapping and rattling down on to the beach. Yet it was not these sounds that had waked him. He lay in the darkness, listening, his head raised and his muzzle sniffing the air. Above the slap and crash of the waves and the murmur of the wind, he heard the sound again, the call of his own kind, yet faint and pitifully weak.

He moaned in answer, and the call came again. Steadily he dragged himself over the stones, making his way across the beach to the clutter of rocks from where the sound came. In a crevice in the rocks he found her, lying quite still, a cow seal that made no effort to move, save to raise a flipper in greeting.

Halic fell asleep again, and when next he woke it was dawn, and he was better able to see the seal that had called in the night. She was extremely emaciated, and her lower jaw hung

loose and broken, shattered by a rifle shot many weeks ago. The original wound had healed, but the jaw was so deformed and useless that she was unable to eat. Halic did not understand, but he stayed by her side, not because of any desire to help, or feeling of pity, but because he himself gained comfort from her presence.

Beneath bushy white eyebrows, a pair of eyes watched the two seals as they lay in the thin light of dawn. The man was old and gaunt, but the eyes were keen, and the hands that held the telescope, though gnarled and bony, were steady. All his life he had been a hunter, climbing far into the mountains in search of deer, bear and lynx. His joy had been in the long stalk and the quick, clean kill.

For days now, ever since he had heard from the fishermen of the plight of this seal, he had sought her, tramping miles along the cliffs, and scanning the sea for hours under the hot sun. Now he had found her, and his quick, indrawn breath told of his disgust and pity as he laid down the telescope and reached for the rifle at his side.

It was a long shot, and a difficult one. With a skill born of long experience he estimated the range and set his sights. The faint click as he eased a cartridge into the breech caused Halic to raise his head, and the old man swore softly as Halic moved into the crossed wires of the telescopic sights, effectively blocking his aim. He lowered the rifle and waited, as the dawn light grew stronger.

Slowly, Halic lowered his head in slumber, and now the hunter had the cow seal in his sights. He drew in a slow breath, cuddled the stock to his cheek, and squeezed the trigger.

With the report, Halic exploded into life. He caught one glimpse of the other seal, as her eyes slowly closed and the fountain of red blood spurted on to the rocks. Then he was gone, the green water closing over his head as he made out to sea.

The hunter watched through his sights as the small spout of blood weakened and finally died away altogether. Then he rose, and made his way slowly back along the cliffs. He was conscious of a strange feeling of satisfaction mingled with emptiness, the ebb tide of emotion known only to those who have loved, and hunters who have killed.

15. The Threat of the Spear

Winter came, and Halic rode the gales far out in the tempestuous waters of the bay of Biscay. The summer population of fishes had gone, the sardine and the tuna, the mackerel and the bass, moving away to their winter quarters far to the west, to gather in readiness for spawning. With them had gone the whales, the dolphins, and the porpoises. Gone too were the tigers of the sea, the sharks—mako and porbeagle, thresher and blue shark. They were all creatures that depended on the plankton bloom, either directly or indirectly, and they were denizens of the upper sunlit waters. Now the sea lay fallow, waiting for the spring.

Yet still there was plenty of food for Halic. Skate and dogfish, conger and pollack, wrasse and whiting, all were hunted down and caught, so that Halic suffered no check in his growth. In fact, he put on weight, so that he was now heavier and stronger than a man, with powerful muscles and jaws like a leopard. He had molted again, losing the faded appearance that had marked him as a yearling, and wore the gray livery of an adult. Slowly he drifted north, and by late spring he had reached that part of Brittany that faces southwest, and found the island which is called Belle Ile.

Here the waves leaped in white fury at the weatherworn rock. The music of the surf roused in Halic strange emotions, feelings of nostalgia and unrest, which he could not understand or relieve in any way. His return to shallow waters, guarded by the high ramparts of the cliffs, amid a pattern of green islands, had evoked half-forgotten memories of home waters. It was, too, the time of the spring gatherings, and unconsciously, Halic sought the company of his own kind.

Throughout the summer Halic slowly journeyed north, following the cliffbound coastline, exploring the small sea with its multitude of tiny islands, on past the peninsula of Quiberon and the islands of de Groix and Glenans. As the long hot summer reached its peak, Halic grew more restless and uneasy. The seas were crowded, not only by the throngs of holidaymakers, English and French, who had come to swim in the warm surf and lie browning on the sun-whitened beaches, but by the red-sailed fishing boats that plied between harbor and sea. On calm days they fished for sardines, baiting the surface of the sea with cod roes and flour, netting the tiny fish as they boiled on the surface, and then hurrying back to port before the catch deteriorated in the heat. Or they fished for tunny, or mackerel, or trawled for turbot and brill.

Halic managed to avoid attracting attention, hugging the high cliffs and staying away from the crowded beaches. He swam deep down, among forests of weed and sponge, where sea horses and pipe fish clung, swaying in the sea as they hunted the small shrimps and fish that were their prey.

A narrow creek of sea thrust landward between black crags, where seabirds mewed and clamored. One claw of rock stretched seaward, breaking the force of the waves and providing shelter for a wealth of life in the deep clear waters of the inlet.

Halic swept in from the sea, swimming on his back, for in this way he was better able to survey the seabed and locate his prey. A shoal of small bass, trapped, were unable to gain the sanctuary of the sea. Halic took three, bolting them down whole, and swallowing them head first so that the spiny dorsal fins did not lacerate his throat. Then he quested around, nosing along the precipitous walls of rock, eagerly seeking fresh prey, for three small fish were less than a snack to him, and merely whetted his appetite.

In a small hollow at the base of the cliff an octopus lay guarding her eggs, which hung like a bunch of bananas from the roof of the miniature cave. The eggs were translucent, about one eighth of an inch in length, and were grouped in clusters, each cluster five inches long, and containing about a thousand eggs. There were over fifty of these clusters, and they had taken the octopus two weeks to lay.

Now she protected them, carefully washing away any debris that threatened to contaminate them, by squirts of water. Until they hatched, and darted away like a host of tiny fleas, the octopus would not feed, and by the time her work was done, she would probably have lost the ability to eat, and so die.

The octopus saw Halic, and paled and fluttered with fear, pressing close into the sheltering cavity in the rock. Halic seized one of her arms and wrenched, with a sudden shake of his head. The octopus held on to her lair, and the arm came away.

Halic swallowed the arm, and swam back. This time he managed to grasp her by the mantle, and with a couple of swift bites, cut into her brain and killed her. Then he surfaced, and tore the cephalopod to pieces, bolting the remnants without attempting to chew them. The eggs in the cave he ignored.

They would survive. Already the embryo cephalopods were showing through the transparent capsules, and in a few days they would hatch. They no longer needed the attention of their parent, and they would drift away, at first over the seabed, eventually to join the plankton, to prey, and be preyed upon.

Halic finished his meal, yawned, rubbed his face with his front flippers, and sank slowly to the bottom of the creek. A few bubbles of air escaped from his nostrils, and rose in a silvery stream to the surface. The tide gently rocked his body, and he slept.

Halic's dealings with the octopus had been watched by a young man who lay on the cliff. The man was a Frenchman, from the suburbs of Paris, and he knew little of the ways of the wild. Pale and dark, with the smooth soft muscles of the townsman, he was himself a hunter of the sea, for each year he came to the coast, and, dressed in a suit of dark rubber, with artificial flippers, a face mask, and twin cylinders of compressed air, he roamed the shallow seas, seeking fish to kill with his spear.

The spear, with its razor-sharp head of steel and shaft of light alloy, he fired from a gun powered by strong bands of rubber. With practice, he had learned to stalk the fish as they swam in the clear waters, until he could draw near enough to fire his spear with deadly accuracy through their silver flanks. Now, as he gazed down at Halic asleep in the limpid waters of the inlet, mixed emotions ran through him.

He had been revolted by the death of the octopus, and Halic's manner of feeding. He thought it wrong that the sea should hold such creatures as seals, which robbed man of the fish that swam there. Above all, his hunting instincts were aroused by the thought of slaying Halic. It would make a wonderful story to tell his friends on return to the city. The pelt would make a handsome rug or bedspread, even, perhaps, a jacket or a pair of shoes.

Excited, he made his way down the cliff, out on to the long arm of rock. Carefully he donned his gear, checked that his armory was correct, and that the long knife he carried was loose in its sheath. Then he entered the water on the seaward side of the rock, and swam quietly round into the inlet.

As yet he could not see Halic. He slid slowly and cautiously over the sea floor, peering ahead into the creek, his gun ready, and his finger curled over the trigger. He breathed slowly,

carefully, struggling to calm his beating heart and still his trembling muscles. A thin stream of bubbles trailed behind him, rising wavering to the surface.

At last he could make out the shape of Halic, a distorted gray form rippling in the waves. A moment of terror surged through the diver, almost causing him to panic and flee. Halic was big, much bigger than he had seemed from the cliff top, bigger than the man himself. For a second, the diver wondered whether he would not be wiser to depart quietly, leaving the seal to sleep in peace, but immediately the instincts of the hunter returned in force. This was a bigger prize than he had imagined.

At that moment Halic stirred, and as the man watched, hypnotized by the strange behavior, Halic sailed languidly to the surface, to breathe.

Foolishly, the man followed, and the disturbance of the water woke Halic, who instantly crash-dived, slapping the sea with one flipper and sprinting up toward the head of the inlet. As he turned, he saw the strange figure of the man, swimming slowly and lumberingly toward him. As detail grew clearer, Halic saw the shining mask, and the white hands, gripping the metal of the gun. Instant recollection came to Halic, and he swerved away, as, in slow motion it seemed, the spear inscribed a gleaming arc through the sea and passed to one side.

Now all Halic wanted to do was to gain the open sea. He swam to bypass the man, but the diver turned to intercept him. Halic saw again the white hand, this time raised in threat, and now armed with the gleam of the knife blade. His jaws closed round the wrist, feeling the wrench and jerk as the diver struggled to free himself, and seeing the knife sink flickering to the seabed as the fingers extended in agony.

Almost fainting with pain, the man sought to grapple with Halic, striving to find some purchase with his free hand on the great bulk which now pounded him on the sea floor and threatened to sever his wrist. Yet Halic had no desire to prolong the fight. He released his hold on the man, chopped once, with terrible force, deep into the muscles of the man's shoulder and neck, and then swam with all speed far out to sea.

Somehow the man regained the rocks. Painfully he divested himself of his gear before losing consciousness. Some hours later he was found by a group of holidaymakers and taken to the hospital, where his wounds were dressed and his shattered nerves treated with sedatives. By the time he had convinced the authorities of the truth of his strange adventure, Halic was fifty miles away from land.

He swam northwest, and at dawn of the third day he came to the Scilly Isles. Here, amid the savage riptides and overfalls that swirled and eddied between the land, he fed for the first time, before hauling out on a sheltered pebble beach, to sleep in the morning sun.

16. Guardian of the Wreck

The sound of seals, sobbing and wailing above the rattle and crash of the waves, roused Halic from slumber. He had slept long, and night was falling. The small beach was shrouded in purple shadow as the sun sank behind the cliffs. In the darkening water two seals played, their dark heads visible in the foam. Halic called in answer, and the seals turned, staring in the direction of the sound, hanging upright and motionless in the sea.

They were yearling cows, cave calves from the rocky fastnesses of North Cornwall, who had strayed south during the summer, meeting by chance in the maze of channels and tide races that intersected the islands. Now they welcomed Halic, and together they played as the ocher moon rose high over the sea.

In the weeks that followed, the trio stayed together, using the same beach and playing in the shallow seas around the island. The yearlings were much smaller than Halic, and were a little in awe of him. They would wrestle and fight, teasing and tormenting him, never allowing him more than the briefest contact, or the smallest intimacy. Always his clumsy attempts at courtship were rejected.

All the while, Halic played at being a beachmaster, guarding his chaste harem against a challenger who never appeared. During the day, when the cows lay hauled out on the stony beach, he spent long hours patrolling to and fro in the sea, his sleek head showing dark above the waves. If a seagull or cormorant landed near, he surged toward it, driving it away from his territory with snapping jaws and angry bark. He never caught one, for the prudent birds took wing long before he got within range.

Each lump of floating driftwood, each cluster of weed or flotsam was carefully checked and investigated. Every unusual sound caused him to hang motionless, upright in the water, listening intently until he was sure all was well. Even when he hauled out, to lie dozing beside the cows on the warm pebbles, he never quite relaxed, raising his head and listening, alert for instant fight or flight, at the rustle of a bird wing, or the tiny scratching of a rabbit in the turf.

When either of the cows left the beach Halic followed her into the waves, staying a discreet distance from her, but keeping her between him and the beach, driving her shoreward if she seemed inclined to stray. Neither of the two cows seemed to resent his behavior in any way. In fact they enjoyed his attentions, deriving comfort and security from his presence, and growing anxious if for some reason he was not close at hand, or immediately visible.

Throughout the autumn, and well into the winter, the weather remained fine and warm, with long days of sunshine and fair winds, which seldom increased to gale force. The fishing was good, for the plankton bloom had persisted for an unusual length of time, and the fish of the summer seas were reluctant to leave such rich pastures. So the seals continued to feed well, for Halic's devotion to duty was not strong enough to affect his appetite. As yet the desire to reproduce his own kind had not grown strong enough to influence his behavior greatly, and his association with the yearlings arose mainly from a desire for companionship.

By December the trio were beginning to drift apart, departing on long lone fishing trips around the islands. From time to time they would return to the beach, but for days at a time they would be out at sea, miles from the nearest land. It was while on one of these trips, when Halic fished at sea ten miles to the west of the islands, that a sudden gale ended their association forever.

The wind blew from the southwest, driving before it mountainous seas that raced landward, to break against the coast of Cornwall. Halic rode out the gale in a fishless, twilit sea. He was carried north and east, past Land's End and Cape Cornwall, until at last the gale abated, and he lay in calmer seas six miles northwest of St. Ives.

Here, more than half a century ago, as Great Britain and the United States of America joined forces in a bid to free Europe from strife, and to win a war that was to end all wars, an admiralty transport vessel of some seven thousand tons was bound from London to Barry, in South Wales. At lunchtime on a day early in December she struck a mine, and as the explosion shook the ship and she began to settle by the stern, the crew took to the boats.

The ship sank quickly, to lie on the stones a hundred feet below the waves. At first she moved her resting place from time to time, as the gales of winter stirred up the seas, but at last the sea claimed her for its own and cemented her firmly into place. Slowly, as she began to rust, as her woodwork rotted and her furnishings decayed, her metallic frame became carpeted with a dense growth of corals and ascidians, sponges and sea fans. The effect was that of some exotic rock garden, planted with ferns and cacti, muting the stark outlines of the wreck.

The wreck became a shelter for shoals of small fishes and crustaceans, shellfish, crabs, and lobsters. Soon the predators found them and moved in, also taking up residence in the wreck. Starfish carpeted the bridge. Small fishes darted in and out of the portholes and hovered on stairway and companionway. An octopus lived in an empty cupboard.

Conger, some of them of immense size, lurked in dark corners, or prowled the man-made caves of the holds. As the years passed, the wreck grew less and less like a ship, and more like a submarine castle, a fortress of stone rising from the seabed, surrounded by shimmering shoals of silver and gold fishes, rising and falling, flickering in the twilight of the tide.

Halic was hungry after his enforced fast in the gale, and he dived down to scour the seabed in search of prey. A fair-sized pollack sheltering near the bows of the wreck fell an easy victim, and he rose to the surface, gripping the struggling fish in his jaws, to take it apart at his leisure. Still hungry, he dived again, skimming along the precipitous wall of the hull, and gliding over the rime-encrusted deck.

Fat pouting hung in streamers by the rigging, and Halic took them as they scattered, crushing each one before swallowing it whole. He caught ten before he felt the need for surfacing again, leaving behind him a trail of glittering silver scales.

Halic dived a third time, still eager to hunt, but now, his appetite somewhat satiated, more in a spirit of exploration. He swam slowly, cruising along the seabed under the overhang of the encrusted hull. Crouched among the crevices in the stones were several large edible crabs, a spider crab, and two lobsters. They lay quietly, waiting for whatever food the turn of the tide might bring them. Apart from large octopuses, they now had few enemies, and all save one had grown too big to fear any danger.

An angler fish lay among the stones, its long tail in a slight curve, and its wide, grotesque head with its enormous mouth partly concealed by the mottled browns and grays of its coloration. Over the years the first ray of its dorsal fin had undergone a curious modification. It had moved forward to the top of the angler's head, and had grown into a rod with a fine line attached. At the end of the line was a little forked fleshy lure, which when the angler waved its fin, darted about like a tiny fish or shrimp.

Small fish were attracted by this lure, but they were never allowed to seize it. Instead, the angler maneuvered the bait so that the fish was positioned with its head down, right in front of the angler's mouth. Suddenly the ferocious jaws would open and snap shut faster than the eye could follow. Next moment the little fish would be gone, trapped in the terrible teeth.

Halic ignored the angler fish. He had eaten them in the past, and although they were easy prey, he found them spiny and unappetizing. He swam on to the stern of the wreck, where a gaping hole showed where the mine had struck. Beyond the opening all was darkness and silence. The jagged entrance was like the jaws of a killer whale, and Halic hesitated, feeling instinctively that somewhere within danger threatened.

At that moment a large, eellike fish appeared, drifting round the stern of the wreck. It was a ling about four feet long, and Halic struck at it as it came within range. At the last moment the ling shot forward, and Halic's jaws closed around its flank and tail, completely severing the caudal fin. Crippled, the ling struggled away, limping down and making for the hole in the wreck.

Halic followed, all his nervousness forgotten in the heat and excitement of the chase, pursuing the wounded fish into the darkness of the hold. Next moment he turned a complete somersault in the water, and without pausing he shot out of the wreck as though he had been fired by a gun, not stopping until he reached the surface a hundred yards away.

In the brief moment that he had stayed in the hold, he had caught a glimpse of eight powerful suckered arms, and two tentacles, surmounted by an enormous eye. Two of the arms had clasped the ling, and bore it toward a giant body which lay shrouded in shadow. Halic's sense of forboding about the wreck had been fully justified.

He had chanced upon the lair of a giant squid, a species normally confined to the deeper waters of the Atlantic, and rarely seen except when injury or violent gales washed them near the shore. Usually they stayed out far beyond the continental shelf, where their only enemies were the whales and killer whales. Sperm whales particularly preyed upon them, often diving to great depths, a thousand fathoms or more, in pursuit.

The one Halic met was quite a small one, with a body some six feet in length, and tentacles almost four times as long. Had Halic entered the hold before the ling he would certainly have been attacked, and he would have stood little chance of survival, in spite of his hasty exit. The squid could have caught up with him without any difficulty at all, so fast could it move.

It had drifted to the wreck on a gale many years ago, and soon would leave its shelter to migrate far out to sea. In time it might grow to a length of more than fifty feet, eventually perhaps to die and be washed up on some mainland beach, to give rise to a fresh crop of stories about sea serpents, and cause some embarrassment to the civic authority who would be obliged to dispose of the carcass.

Halic had no desire to explore the wreck further. He swam out to sea, away from the wreck and the distant coastline. The wind was beginning to rise again, sweeping with violent gusts across the face of the angry sea. Far away, massed on the horizon, lay convoluted banks of dark cloud, pillowing into the sky. Behind them the sun set silver, and from time to time ragged black fragments of cloud would be lit with white fire as they detached themselves from the mass, to come racing over the sky like the advance scouts of some invading army.

They brought with them stinging arrows of hail and cold rain, lashing the sea for a brief moment as they passed. By nightfall the battalions of the cloud legions were massed from horizon to horizon, and over the land snow fell, blotting out all detail and blanketing all sound.

Halic slid deep under the waves and slept, to dream uneasily of young maiden seals. In his sleep he saw the yellow-walled cliffs of his birth, and the black pillars of rock where the golden pollack played. He heard the hiss of spray as the mackerel swept through the sound, and saw the slow curl of dark bodies as the porpoise followed. Above all he heard the call of his kind, beckoning him back to the waters of his birth.

17. *Return to the Islands*

Spring came early to the Pembroke coast, and warm rain plumped the dry acid soil of the cliff tops. Faint flushes of newer, paler green lit the carpets of heather and blueberries, and the deep gold of the gorse was reflected in the waxy petals of the primrose. Wild daffodils nodded beneath the bare branches of trees where thrushes sang in the soft evening light.

The night skies were alive with the flutter of bird wings, as swallows and martins, wagtails and warblers, travelers from the far south, mingled with the throngs of winter visitors, fieldfares, starlings, bramblings and redwings, departing for the north and east.

Many of the birds did not survive the ordeal. Some, blown off course by high winds, flew on over open seas, until, exhausted and far from land, they dropped to their death in the waves. Others crashed into the rigging of ships, and hundreds more were lured by the flashing lights of lighthouses around the coasts, flying straight into the glare of the lantern, so that they were dashed against the glass, to fall broken on to the rocks below. Still the survivors pressed on, driven by a compulsion beyond human comprehension, and oriented by some means as yet unsolved by mankind.

Halic heard the travelers pass overhead as he journeyed through the darkness, and from time to time he came upon the corpses of casualties, sodden bundles of feathers floating in the waves. Once more Halic was far out at sea, heading north to return again to the island of his birth, swimming steadily and purposefully, as if drawn by a magnet to the coastline of Wales.

He passed great rafts of puffins, floating on the rise and fall of the Atlantic swell. They were handsome birds, in their neat pied plumage, but their enormous technicolored bills, barred with bands of vermilion, gray, and white, gave them a clownish appearance. Ever since the previous August they had stayed far out at sea, fishing and riding out the winter gales. The young birds were spending their second winter at sea, after an absence from land of almost two years. Now they were gathering in readiness for their return to their ancestral breeding grounds, in burrows at the top of the cliffs.

Halic passed them by, and the puffins hardly troubled to move out of his way. The birds were used to the seals and did not fear them. Occasionally Halic made a halfhearted lunge at one which fluttered enticingly in front of him, but always in the nick of time the bird flew up out of reach, to pitch down in the waves a few yards away. Soon Halic had left the puffins far behind, but at dawn the next day they caught up with him and overtook him, flying past on whirring wings. They reached the land long before he did.

Halic could smell the land now. The wind was laden with the scent of gorse and newly turned soil, wet rocks and seaweed. He quickened his speed, dipping down under the surface of the sea and swimming effortlessly on, hour after hour, as the day passed and the night rolled slowly by.

In the pale light of a spring dawn, as the sun sent yellow shafts of light slanting on to the beach, a young cow seal idled on the edge of the tide. Her name was Lugo, and she was a cave calf, born in the darkness of the mainland cliffs across the Sound from the beach where Halic had spent the first weeks of his life. She was a year younger than he, and very palely marked, the silver of her back being but lightly speckled with gray.

A yellow ball came drifting by on the ebb, a plastic marker which had broken adrift from a fishing net. Lugo followed it, pushing it around in the waves and diving under it to balance it on her head. She tried several times to grasp it in her jaws, but it was too large for her, and the smooth round surface offered no purchase to her teeth.

The ball flowed swiftly on the ebbing tide, and she followed it down to the mouth of the Sound, where the sea foamed over the hidden rocks. Far out in the bay a small black dot appeared, a dot which disappeared from time to time below the waves. Each time it resurfaced it grew nearer, until at last the two seals met. The newcomer was larger and darker than Lugo, and she at once accepted him and allowed him to join in her game. As he rolled in the sea a small white scar showed on his neck. Halic, the wanderer, had come home from the sea.

For a while they played together, but Halic was weary, and longed for sleep. He swam away, and Lugo abandoned her toy, following him as he swam north up the Sound. Together they hauled out on the beach where he had been born, and Halic promptly fell into a deep slumber. Lugo lay beside him, gazing round her with wide, dark eyes, content for the moment to enjoy the warmth of the morning sun, and to watch the other seals that lay hauled out on the beach.

Once again it was the time of the spring gatherings, and the seals had assembled for the ritual and pleasure of the courtship dances. An immense bull lay where the ebbing tide had stranded him on a rock, the craggy outline of his head silhouetted against the sky. A group of cows sprawled on the stones, irritably repulsing the halfhearted overtures of a young bull who, each time he was rebuffed, retired hastily, waving a placatory fore flipper. At last, sulkily, he meandered down to the edge of the tide, and fell asleep in the shallow water. Lugo and Halic were the only adolescent seals on the beach.

In the late afternoon a chough flew low over the cliff on ragged black wings, his beak and legs shining cherry red in the sun. Once his numbers had haunted the cliff tops along the entire coastline of Cornwall, but now the choughs had vanished from those shores, and only here in the wild lands of Pembroke did they survive in any strength. As he swept over the turf in search of beetles and lizards his harsh scream woke Halic, who yawned and stretched, his body curving into a crescent, his head and tail raised high above the stones.

Lugo followed him into the sea, and together they went fishing out in the bay. It was too early for mackerel, but dense shoals of plaice were moving north to their spawning grounds off the Cardiganshire coast. Halic and Lugo fed well, picking out the larger fish, those between three and four pounds in weight, and bearing them to the surface to tear them apart.

During the weeks that followed they were seldom apart, fishing and playing together, and spending long hours on the beach, sleeping and sunbathing, as the days grew longer and the sea warmer.

Over all lay the power of spring. It exuded from the pale light of the sun and the warm breath of the salty wind. It shone from the bright eye of the adder coiled among the heather roots, and glistened on the watery backs of the spawning frogs. It echoed from the hum of busy insects and the laughing cry of the gulls. It penetrated the dark earth and lit the dark waters, so that they burgeoned with life. It had an intoxicating force that no creature could deny.

The wine of spring flowed in the blood of the seals, and sent Halic and Lugo racing and plunging through the sea, calling to each other and chasing each other through the waving forests of kelp. Their games reflected their exuberance, and also their high degree of intelligence. Halic would find a piece of driftwood, and dive down into the sea, clutching the wood between his jaws. Lugo would follow, and deep down Halic would release his prize. Then the two seals would race after it as it rocketed to the surface, striving to catch it before it broke the surface of the waves.

Sometimes he would loll in the waves, holding a stick in his jaws, enticing Lugo to come and take it away. As she drew near he would fling it away with a shake of his head, and then both seals would launch themselves after it, each striving to be the first to reach the prize. If, as usually happened, Halic was first to reach the stick, he would race away with it clasped in his jaws, while Lugo would follow in hot pursuit. At other times both seals would arrive at the goal together, and then the stick would be forgotten as they locked in mock combat, wrestling and rolling in the waves.

Then the seals would be aroused by strange emotions that they did not understand or know how to satisfy. At such times Halic would try to grasp Lugo by the nape of her neck, embracing her with his flippers, while Lugo, half excited and half fearful, would turn to face him, nibbling at his face and neck until he was forced to release her. Next moment they would be racing away through the waves, their desires forgotten. Their relationship remained chaste, although the alchemy of love was beginning to stir within them.

Their parting, when it came, was sudden and unexpected. Halic had found a lumpsucker stranded by the tide. These obese, ungainly fish laid vast numbers of pink eggs in the spring, in shallow water at the edge of the low tide mark. Then the males stayed to guard the eggs, anchoring themselves to the stones by means of a powerful sucker on their undersides, and remaining at their posts even though half exposed to the air.

Halic was hungry, and when Lugo came to join him he growled a warning to her, telling her to keep away as he bit and worried at the fish, still clinging grimly to its stone.

Innocently, Lugo ignored the warning, and came closer, whereupon Halic snapped at her, and, taken by surprise, she bit back. By an unlucky chance, she caught Halic neatly on the nose, drawing blood. Berserk with pain and rage, Halic flung himself at her, rolling her over and over into the waves. Terrified, Lugo fled, and as Halic returned, grumbling, to the lumpsucker, she swam away down the Sound. At the south of the island she fell in with a band of adolescent seals, and with them drifted away to the rocks that lay to the west. Soon she had forgotten all about Halic.

18. Bachelor Days

The summer seas were infinitely more crowded and busy than they were in winter. As well as the resident populations of seals, birds, and fishes, visitors of all species came to sea and shore, cliff top and beach. Not least of these were the humans, as with increased leisure and prosperity, they were able to follow the new motorways in search of unspoiled, uncrowded areas in which to spend their holidays.

Perversely, they then flocked to the beaches, and only a comparative few explored far along the cliff tops. In the small harbors, pleasure craft occupied every vacant berth among the fishing boats, but few amateur sailors ventured into the Sound, with its hidden reefs, its dangerous tide races, and sudden overfalls. It seemed that the humans, like seals, were gregarious, and sought company as long as their privacy was not jeopardized. While they wished to enjoy an environment which was wild and untamed, they still needed the reassurance afforded by the close proximity of their kind. In fact, the pattern of human behavior on the beaches as the tide rose was not dissimiliar to that of the seals, as elderly matrons moved unwillingly away from the sea, and scolded those adolescents whose boisterous play interfered with their slumbers.

The seals had their own private beaches, on which they were little disturbed. Each day during the summer months, the seals would awake to the throb of diesel engines, as small boats nosed slowly and quietly along the shoreline. Certain fisher-men, more astute than the rest, had discovered that rather than spend long, arduous hours fishing for mackerel and lobsters, it was more profitable and pleasurable to take boatloads of visitors to view the seabirds and seals.

Since the appearance of the boats was harmless, and since nothing happened to harm the seals, they gradually grew ac-customed to the repeated visits, merely raising their heads enquiringly as the boats slid past. Even Halic, who viewed boats, along with all things pertaining to mankind, with deep suspicion, slowly became used to them, although if he were near the water's edge, he would slip nervously into the sea and remain underwater until any possible danger had passed.

Fishermen still set their lobster pots near the islands during the calm days of summer. The "pots" were in fact cages made from a wooden framework, clad with netting of wire or nylon. Once the pots had been woven, like baskets, from slender wands of willow, but latterly this method had proved too expensive and tedious. Each pot was tied to a long line, weighted with a stone so that it would sink right way up, and baited with a piece of fresh mackerel secured on a spike. A narrow, funnel-shaped aperture allowed entrance, but no es-cape.

At one time, seabirds were used as bait, and perhaps the older fishermen, when catches were poor, looked longingly at the birds that were now protected by law, and wished that they could return to the ways of their youth.

As well as lobsters, the pots caught spider crabs and conger eels, prawns and edible crabs. The fishermen smashed the spider crabs on the gunwales of the boat, and speared the eels with their knives. Sometimes the pots brought up starfish, and again the fishermen mutilated these unwanted captives, de-claring them the vermin of the sea. Very often, in chopping up starfish, the fishermen were merely increasing their numbers, for each leg with a portion of body attached would, when thrown back into the sea, grow to be another starfish.

Squid and cuttlefish robbed the pots, and sometimes a large shoal of them would raid a string of pots, taking every bait before the lobsters had time to find it. Sometimes Halic, attracted by a writhing conger or octopus, would break open a pot and remove the trespasser.

Certainly the tourist trade was more dependable than lobster fishing, and, though subject to the vagaries of the weather, more lucrative. Besides, as one man pointed out, there was no need to load or unload the catch. The boat emptied and filled itself!

For many of the holidaymakers the seals and the seabirds were the object of their visit. Coming from town and city, preoccupied with the necessity of earning a living and raising a family for most of the year, they looked forward to nothing more than a chance to rest, to enjoy unpolluted air, and to watch and admire creatures free and at large in this rugged setting. Their minds, as well as their bodies, needed this period of rest and regeneration.

Halic spent long hours, when he was not fishing, in lying on the beaches and rocks, basking in the warm sun. Like all seals, he had an infinite capacity for sleep, and gave the appearance of enjoying to the full the drowsiness that overtook him. He lay on beach or rock, his coat dry and brown with the sun, yawning and stretching, idly scratching his sleek hide with a lazy fore flipper. Then he would smack his lips contentedly, his heavy eyelids would droop, and his head would sink gently on to the stones. When, as happened at times, the sun grew too hot for him, he would slip into the shallow water at the edge of the tide and continue his slumbers beneath the waves, rocked by the gently rolling surf.

As the summer died, the visitors began to slip away. The swallows that had skimmed the cliffs departed for the south, and the holidaymakers returned to the towns. The hotels closed, and the boats lay shrouded on the quaysides. Soon the only traces left by the holidaymakers would be a child's plastic bucket half buried by the tide, and patches of worn turf on the cliff tops.

On the beaches the fat white calves lay beside their mothers, and the adult bulls patrolled the tideline, roaring their defiance at any trespasser. Soon winter would come, and the beaches would lie abandoned by all save the rolling surf and the mewing gulls.

As the plankton bloom expired, the mackerel began to drift away south. The bass and mullet lingered on, but soon they too would be gone. As the seas grew colder, the fish that had thronged in the shallower water began to move out to the depths. The seals followed them. Gradually, the cows abandoned their weaned calves, leaving them to a winter of solitude and fasting. The mothers enjoyed a brief spell of courtship with the bulls, before heading out to sea. The beachmasters followed the last cows away from land, and the calves were washed off the beaches, or swam away of their own free will.

Only occasionally would a seal haul out on a beach in winter, and then only for a brief period, in calm, sunny weather. Most of the time the beaches were wild, inhospitable places, lashed by storm-driven waves and showers of cold, stinging rain. Not until the following spring would the seals reclaim the beaches for their annual gatherings.

Halic rode out the wild gales of midwinter in deep water, sometimes rocked by the waves, sometimes sinking deep down into calm waters where the kelp waved languidly, and the light was dim. In his pattern of existence time was of no importance. Whether it was night or day was a matter of small consequence, and the slow changes of the seasons made little difference to him.

In more settled weather the seals returned to the coasts, appearing offshore at the foot of the high cliffs, nosing among the beards of wrack and kelp, and lounging nonchalantly in the white backwash of the waves, or riding the green crests of the groundswell as it rolled in from the Atlantic. They did not stay for long, however, and disappeared as quietly and mysteriously as they had arrived.

19. Death of a Huntress

To the south of the Sound, where the narrow channel cut by the tide widened out into the sandy bed of the bay, the sloping seabed was a mixture of stones and gravel, sand and broken shell, giving way to rock. Just opposite the most southerly of the stacks and islets that lay scattered around the island, on the other side of the channel, lay a wide depression in the seabed, some thirty feet deeper than the surrounding floor.

Into this hollow the tide brought a constant supply of rotting debris, which was converted by the marine life into a rich supply of fish food. Here the bottom-living fish congregated, browsing over the submarine valley in dense packs, and in turn providing food themselves. Halic visited the spot throughout the year, and seldom went away hungry.

On a gusty morning in May, a stranger came to the Sound. Halic spotted her as he swam in the sea off the Porth Clais Rock, a female tope. She was a magnificent specimen of her kind, and her long, gray, sharklike form cut the water with a speed and grace surpassing that of Halic's.

In the weeks that followed she was seen by most of the inhabitants of the Sound. From the cliff tops the ravens and the seabirds saw her cruising along below the surface of the clear water, and from time to time the seals saw her crescent-shaped fin, cutting like a knife through the waves. Most of the time, however, she kept deep down, hugging the sandy bed of the sea, for her prey was fish, particularly the bony flatfish that abounded in this part of the bay. She established a regular patrol, from the Porth Clais Rock to Sylvia Rock, circling out to sea and then back again. She soon discovered the hollow in the seabed.

The next time Halic visited the depression he found it deserted, save for the presence of a skate weighing over a hundred pounds, lying inert on the floor of the sea, and a pair of small dogfish, which fled in panic at his approach. For days previously, a reign of terror had ruled, as every few hours the gray huntress had swept into the crater, chopping and carving the ranks of the helpless flatfishes, until now the survivors were scattered far and wide over the bay. Mystified, Halic swam away, to seek better hunting grounds among the rocks.

A white cruiser came purring across the bay. Though small, she was sturdy, and well equipped, and in the little cabin that lay forward near the bows, two men studied the flickering red line on the echo sounder. They were deep-sea anglers, and they were using the latest equipment to try and locate the hollow. Slowly they cruised to and fro, until suddenly the navigator showed they were passing over deeper water. As the needle began to rise again, the man at the helm put the boat into reverse, and when they were once more over the pit the other man dropped a yellow marker overboard. Attached to the marker was a weight on a long line, so having located the fishing ground, the men sailed the boat a few yards uptide of the hollow, and dropped anchor.

Earlier, they had spent some time fishing with handlines, catching a supply of fresh mackerel to use as bait. The lines were attached to heavy sinkers, and hung with hooks dressed with brightly colored feathers, which were attached to the main line with short snoods of nylon. The handlines were jigged up and down in the water, and the suicidal mackerel, imagining the dancing, flashing feathers to be small fish, struck at them to be impaled on the hooks. Any number, from six to a dozen, might be caught at once in this way, and placed in a bucket. Now they lay, their bright colors fading, carefully covered with a damp cloth to protect them from the sun and wind.

Before they started fishing the two men had checked and rechecked every item of their tackle. Their rods of hollow fiber glass, and the large center pin reels that held hundreds of yards of transparent monofilament line were the best that money could buy. Knots were scientifically tied, and then tested for strength. Hooks were made needle sharp. Each swivel was tested and oiled, and the sinker chosen was of just sufficient weight to hold the bait against the pull of the tide. Two gaffs lay to hand, sharpened ready to land the fish the men hoped to catch. For years they had studied every aspect of their hobby, and left as little as possible to chance.

Now each man chose a mackerel, and with a razor-sharp knife cut a fillet from the whole of one side of the fish. Carefully, the fillets were threaded on to the stainless steel hooks, and the tackle lowered over the side of the boat. Now the tide took the bait, stretching out the long flowing trace, and, as the men paid out line, carried the baits down to the hollow. The men checked the descent of the baits, for they knew that to let the sinker fall too swiftly meant that the bait would wrap itself round the line, and the tackle would drop on the seabed in a hopeless tangle too close to the boat.

The big skate, which Halic had seen in the hollow, was no longer there. The skate was carnivorous, and needed many small flatfishes and crabs to satisfy its bulk. Its small mouth meant that it could not devour large prey, so now it had gone in search of small plaice which lay buried in the sand in the shallow waters of the bay. The two baits lay ignored in the hollow, and for hundreds of yards in every direction the sea was devoid of life.

Although the two men in the boat were father and son, and shared a common interest in this sport of deep-sea angling, they were, both physically and mentally, remarkably dissimilar. The older man was short and stocky, with a bush of iron gray hair that fringed sun-creased features, brown and hard. He was impatient, pragmatic, interested only in results and soon bored with inactivity. The beauty of his surroundings, and the calm and purity of the seascape were, in the absence of fish, of no interest to him.

Now he grumbled, sitting hunched over his rod, and staring at the taut line that stretched down into the tide. "There's no fish here. Two hours without a bite! It was a darned fool idea in the first place. We should be fishing the storm beaches for bass on a day like this."

The son made no answer. He sat sprawled back in his chair, his long lean body stretched out to the sun, and a lock of lank black hair shading his eyes. He was content to dream, to watch the dappled reflection of the waves on the black rocks, and to admire the translucent white of a gull's wing, as it passed against the sun. Now he watched the black oval of a seal's head as it hung in the surge of a breaking wave. He hoped his father wouldn't spot it.

"Look at that old villain! That's why we aren't catching any fish. Wish I had a rifle with me. I'd put a shot across his bows. Look at him, will you? Look what he's got. . . . Vermin!"

Halic lay close to the rocks, tearing the living flesh from the gold flank of a pollack. Earlier he had swum upside down over the hollow, and seen the shimmering strips of mackerel, shying away from the barely visible lines that hung in the sea. Now he bit deep into the pollack, pushing the fish away from his jaws with his front flippers, meantime keeping a wary eye on the boat and its occupants.

Still the son made no comment. Something about the seal, the shape of its head, the burning binocular stare of the large dark eyes, the gesture of pushing the fish away with its flippers, some feature, he knew not what, prompted an odd train of thought. "Was old Darwin right?" he pondered. "Did man really descend from the trees, or did he come out of the sea?"

He half smiled at the thought, part fanciful, part serious, of a species of mammal which, like the seal, had adopted the sea as its environment, but which had not progressed so far. In his mind's eye he saw sunlit, tropical shores washed by warm seas, and a breed of animals, monkeylike, their bodies immersed up to their waists, foraging among the weed-covered rocks. Their flat feet, with prehensile toes, gave them secure footing in the water. Their long, mobile fingers were ideal for probing among the rocks.

Their upright posture was easy to maintain when supported by the sea, and the females could feed their young while in the water, as their breasts were situated high on their chests. They had no need of hair, save on their heads, to protect them from the sun. They could swim well from birth, and unlike most mammals, shared with the seal the ability to swim underwater. Their collarbones had developed as a result of climbing rocks and cliffs after birds' eggs.

"It all fits," the young man thought, continuing to watch Halic as he rode the white swell that surged round the foot of the rocks. "It all ties in, even to our liking for shellfish. How else would man even get to taste such an article, let alone grow to like it? It might even account for the shape of our teeth, which are quite unlike those of other mammals."

Halic had disappeared by now, melting into the waves, but the young fisherman dreamed on, rapt in contemplation of his theory. "Was man once a littoral mammal? What drove him inland—a fall in temperature? He should have had a layer of blubber. Far too many people have that today, fat they could well do without. Perhaps . . . !"

"WAKE UP! YOU'RE ON!"

His reverie shattered by the old man's shout, the son came back to reality with a jolt. The tip of the rod was nodding and jerking as though alive, and the drum of the reel revolved slowly as the line paid out. Carefully he picked up the rod, inserted the butt in the harness he wore round his waist, and let the fish run. Slowly but steadily the reel picked up speed, and he let it go, just keeping enough brake on it to prevent an overrun. Fifty yards went out, seventy-five, then a hundred.

Deep down the tope ran like a gray ghost over the sunlit amber sand. She had picked up the mackerel strip and now held it between her jaws, crushing it slowly with her teeth. Now, with a last savage bite, she gulped the bait back.

As the line stopped running out and the reel slowed to a stop, the fisherman set the check on the reel, adjusted the star drag, and, tightening the slight slack in the line, set the hook, jerking the rod upward until he lay far back in his seat. Then, dropping the rod, he wound in as much line as he could gain, and as he felt the distant lunge and surge of power, he let the curve of the rod take the strain, and heard the rising scream of the reel as the tope began its first run. He knew better than to try and stop it, for the first strike had told him he was into no mean fish, and although the line had a breaking strain of thirty pounds when wet, he was taking no chances.

The instant the tope felt the first jar and wrench of the penetrating hook, she exploded in a burst of panic and energy which sent her scorching far out to sea. As she slowed, she felt a heavy pull which turned her sideways, bringing her veering back toward the boat at a speed little less than her first run. As she came, the fisherman cranked wildly at his reel, desperately anxious that the line should not go slack. The large drum of the reel helped him gain line rapidly, but he was only half prepared for the sickening jolt and thump that came as the tope turned yet again. His rod bent until the tip touched the sea, and the knuckles of his right hand came down on the gunwale with a sickening crunch.

In spite of the pain, he managed to stop winding, and let the fish run. Now she came rocketing to the surface, and the two men gasped as for a brief moment they saw her silhouette against the sky, her wildly thrashing tail threatening to sever the line. Next moment she was down again, zigzagging through the waves and shaking her head in an effort to throw the hook.

Each jolting jar communicated itself to the rod, and the straining arms and shoulders of the man at the rod. Now the tope settled down to sulky, boring runs, each of short duration, but savage and full of power, so that pump as he might, the fisherman could gain no more line. Solicitous, his father bathed his brow, and as the minutes stretched into an hour bound his bleeding knuckles with a cloth dipped in sea water.

Now at last the fish seemed to be weakening. From time to time she came to the surface, but she leaped no more, merely half rolling, with a lazy flap of her tail. Slowly she gave way, and as the line inched on to the reel she drew nearer the boat. Still she was not quite defeated, and as she caught sight of her captors she plunged again, swimming away at a speed that brought a smell of hot oil from the reel. The burst of energy was short-lived, and now she could do little except roll feebly as she was drawn through the water.

At last she lay dead on the deck of the boat, and her captor sat nursing his injured hand, staring at her corpse as his father raised the anchor and set the boat leaping at full throttle across the bay. In time he would relive the excitement of the battle. He would enjoy the rewards of his angling success, as his capture brought him trophies and prizes. But for now, he felt only a deep depression, coupled with remorse at being the killer of such a magnificent specimen. His hand hurt. It was swelling badly, for several small bones were broken, and he was unable to move his fingers. As he fumbled with his left hand to light a cigarette, he heard his father singing at the wheel.

20. *Courtship*

It was September, and Halic swam through the calm water of the Sound, heading for the small, stony beach where already two cows lay with their calves. He was now in his sixth year, and although he had not yet attained his full growth, he weighed well over five hundred pounds, lean, muscular, and powerful.

For some time he had felt strangely ill at ease. During the spring gathering, as he had sported with other seals of his age, he had been prone to sudden outbursts of anger, attacking other bachelor seals with a savage aggression not normally expected at that time. He would fall prey to sudden fits of jealousy, followed by long periods when he would hunt alone, morose and sullen. The other seals began to avoid him, splitting up and abandoning their games when he appeared.

Now, as he thrust through the sea toward the breeding beach the sight of the master bull, patrolling off shore, angered him, and sent him surging forward in defiance of the angry roar that greeted him. They met in a welter of foam, both rearing half out of the water, as with bared teeth they feinted and sparred, each trying to throw the other off guard, to seize the unguarded moment when the other's throat was exposed and bared.

Halic struck first, but the older bull twisted sideways at the last moment, and Halic's teeth sank into the tough hide at the

back of his neck. Now the two of them rolled over and over in the shallow water, until the older, heavier bull tore free.

The speed of the beachmaster, as he returned to the attack, took Halic by surprise. He had a fleeting glimpse of the old bull rearing out of the water, angry eyes staring and white teeth menacing, his mane fringed with a halo of red. Then he felt a violent blow over his heart, and as he sank below the waves he felt the beachmaster's teeth sink into his neck. A ponderous weight forced him down, until his back scraped on the rocks that littered the seabed. He felt himself shaken and pummeled as he twisted and writhed in a frantic effort to break free.

Suddenly, his anger was gone, replaced by fear as he acknowledged the older bull's superiority and added weight. With one last desperate effort he broke free and fled, his body thrashing the waves to foam as his blood streamed out behind him on the tide. The older bull pursued him, but seeing that Halic was vanquished, he soon gave up the chase, and returned to the beach.

Halic swam more slowly now, but he did not stop until he reached the southern tip of the island. Then he hauled out on a flat rock exposed by the ebbing tide, and slept off the strain of his exertions. His wound bled slowly, the blood trickling down the stones and through the waves.

He woke feeling better. His wound had stopped bleeding, and although his neck was stiff, and his chest still hurt where the bull had hit him over the heart, he felt hungry and alive. He slid into the sea and went fishing, his wound stinging from the cleansing action of the salt water. The mackerel were feeding, oblivious to everything except the dense shoal of sand eels that they had found, and Halic took six of their number without alarming the rest of the fish. Then he slept again for a while, hanging bolt upright in the waves, and when he awoke all pain was gone.

During the next few days he stayed at the south end of the

island, fishing among the stacks and rocks that reared skyward from the sea. He was alone, for most of the younger seals were away at sea, and only the cows about to give birth lay on the breeding beaches alongside those that had already calved. The master bulls, those older seals that had claimed their territories earlier in the month, ceaselessly patrolled the shores, forbidding any unattached bull the right of way.

It was the time of the spring tides, and at night Halic played in the moon shadows cast by the high rocks. Across the bay the moon cast a pathway of milky light over the dark carpet of the sea. It was on this pathway that Halic first saw her, her neat round head silver in the moonlight. She waited as he swam toward her, watching with calm assured eyes the widening vee of his approach. As they met their muzzles touched, briefly, in a seal's greeting. Then she turned and swam slowly away, while Halic followed and drew alongside her. Together they roamed through the milky sea, and from time to time her flank would touch his. Then he would be filled with a fierce desire for possession, so that he would swim over her, trying to grasp the nape of her neck with his strong white teeth. Each time she evaded his embrace, turning toward him so that their faces met in playful bites of love.

Time had dulled memory and blunted recognition, so that the two seals did not remember that once before, long ago, they had played together as they did now. Halic and Lugo, who as a young maiden seal had welcomed him on his return from the sea, were together again.

Day followed night, and as Halic grew more demanding, so she became bolder and more seductive. Still she was not yet ready to consummate their love, and although she continued to excite and arouse him with her charms, she would not straight away give herself in final surrender. As the late summer sun lit the sea, she swam with him through sparkling wavelets, or led him deep down, through brown fronds of waving kelp.

Everywhere she went Halic followed her, by now in a constant fever to possess her. Now she let him clasp her by the skin of her neck, gripping her gently but firmly with his jaws, as his flippers enfolded her warm body. Several times she permitted this, but each time, as he curved his body for the final act of love she broke away and fled, leaving him breathless and shouting as he surged after her through the green sea.

After one such chase as they hung languidly in the waves, a little apart, and for the moment calm and relaxed after the fire and excitement of the past few moments, they were suddenly aware of the presence of a third seal. The stranger swam straight up to Lugo, and, as she turned away startled, he attempted to grasp her by the back of her neck.

Halic came awake with a roar of rage that sent the seabirds whirling like snowflakes round the cliffs. Leaping clear out of the water Halic hit the stranger so hard on the flank that he sank below the surface in a silver cloud of bubbles and spray. As he surfaced, Halic lunged open-mouthed, sinking his teeth deep and spinning round in the water in a savage attempt to tear out the other's throat.

His grip broke, and as the stranger turned to flee Halic crushed one of his fore flippers in one bone-shattering bite. Then the stranger was gone, diving below the waves and swimming fast and far, away from Halic's terrible wrath. Halic watched him go, and then, satisfied that he had conquered, he turned back to Lugo. She was swimming away from him, slowly, with many a backward glance and swerve of her flanks. Halic followed, making no effort to catch her, into the green shadow of a tall underwater cave.

There she waited for him, and, still filled with the pride of battle, he took her, at first roughly and savagely, so that she moaned with the pain of his entry. Slowly he calmed down, to become more gentle and loving, so that all was fluid and light. The clean cold sea was their marriage couch, and the cave their bedchamber, and there, still united in the act of love, they slept in the sea.

That night, as the moon rose with the tide, the sea was lit with blue-green fire. Every wavelet had a phosphorescent fringe, and where the waves broke the rocks shone green in the dark. As Halic and Lugo swam out of the cave, their bodies glowed with the fire and the wake of their passing lit a green trail through the darkness of the sea. Together they danced through the cold flames, and the faster they moved, the brighter the fires glowed.

The phosphorescence was caused by the presence in the autumn plankton bloom of a tiny animal, a dinoflagellate called noctiluca. Each individual was about one sixteenth of an inch in length, and when agitated, it gave off the brilliant blue-green light which gave it its name. There were millions of them present in the sea around the island, and every tiny movement of the water caused them to glow.

In the days that followed, Halic and Lugo repeatedly en-acted their rites of love, at times briefly and spontaneously, at others, especially after a prolonged spell of petting and flirta-tion, slowly and leisurely, so that the minutes drifted on into an hour or more, and still they lay united, at times slipping into slumber, only to reawake and, by soft gentle movements regain those heights of rapture to which they had previously climbed. Each night, so long as the invasion of noctiluca per-sisted, they danced the fire dance. Once, swimming like green ghosts far out in the bay, they came upon a shoal of fish, each lit with the same blue-green glow, and each leaving the same trail of fire.

The seals fed for the first time since they had met. Their teeth and tongues shone, and Halic and Lugo were enchanted by the novelty of this strange, illuminated world, and by their own, uncanny appearance. When dawn came and the phos-phorescence gave way to the more powerful light of the sun, the two seals slept, satiated with love and good food.

Slowly, as the green fire of the noctiluca died, so the fires of passion in Lugo and Halic began to dwindle and fade. Winter was coming. It was announced by the urgent whistle of the curlew as they flew away from the shores, seeking the water-logged meadows inland. It was echoed by the wild geese, as with nightly clamor they flew in from the Northlands, away from the grip of the ice and snow. The mackerel knew, and followed the basking sharks that had lain all summer off the islands. The nights grew colder, and the bracken on the cliff tops turned, first yellow, then russet red.

Gradually, Halic and Lugo drifted apart. Their way was not the way of mankind, or other mammals that mated for life, or shared the duties of a home and the raising of their offspring. Halic would in all probability never see or recognize his calf, and in another year Lugo would be wooed and possessed by whichever bull held the beach or cave which she chose for the calf to be born. This was the way of the seals, and it was a good way, for it ensured the survival of the race.

Although their love was brief and transient, it was none the less deep and true. It was all the more magical because it could happen only once. In another year Halic would most likely win and claim his own breeding beach, to share his desires among several females, not of his own choosing. Lugo would forever be tied to the yearly cycle of calving and pregnancy. This was the one time when she could love without the distracting presence of a calf. Now it was over, and the wind that blew across the sere grass of the headlands was cold and harsh.

21. The Brothers

At the entrance to the cove a line of corks, rocking gently in the rhythmical rise and fall of the swell, marked the site of a drift net, laid earlier in the evening, just as the ebbing tide had turned and begun to flow back into the Sound. Now, at intervals, the corks jerked and bobbed as fishes, swimming into the cove, became trapped while trying to swim out again to sea.

The smaller fishes passed straight through the net. Others, mackerel, mullet, pollack, and bass found that their heads would pass through the mesh of the net, but that their bodies were too large. When they tried to withdraw, their gills became entangled with the nylon cords, and after a brief struggle they suffocated, their gills torn and broken by the net.

Now in the darkest hour of the night the corks once more became agitated, twitching violently, and sometimes disappearing below the surface of the waves. A young seal had found the net, and was stuffing himself as fast as he could bolt the fish down. When he had gorged until he could eat no more, he fell asleep, cradled on the rocky bed of the cove. He was still there at dawn, as the fine wreaths of mist vanished with the sun, and September light flooded the island.

The throb of diesel engines woke him, and he surfaced to breathe, just before the boat appeared round the headland. Now he dived again, only to find his exit to the sea blocked by the approaching boat. He could have passed with safety under the boat, but the tide had ebbed, leaving little depth of water, and so he panicked, first swimming back into the cove toward the beach, and then back out to sea. In his haste he swam straight into the net, to become enveloped in its restricting folds.

To the two men in the boat, who had now picked up both ends of the net, the sudden jarring and jerking told its own story. They did not need to feel the extra weight to know they had caught a seal. One of them nodded grimly to the other, who picked up a heavy wrench, and laid it close at hand on the thwart.

The men were brothers, farmers in a small way, and handicapped and impoverished by lack of capital. To help eke out their limited resources, they were part-time fishermen, and later in the day they would load what fish they had caught into a van, and travel from door to door, selling the fish direct to the customer. Long hours of physical toil had made them tough and hard, and their life of poverty had embittered them, making them resentful of authority, or anyone who was in any way superior to them. The younger of the two had an artificial leg, the result of an accident with a tractor some years before. This fact in itself made him the more sour of the two.

Now, laboriously, they hauled on the net, each silent, yet occupied by the same thought. Instead of a good catch of fish, the proceeds of which would have bought them an evening at the local inn, a chance to escape their dreary existence for an hour or two in a golden haze of beer fumes, they were going to land a worthless seal. Now revenge was all that they could look forward to.

The net was almost all in the boat, and the seal thrashed on the surface as it struggled to free itself. In the end it almost escaped, and it was half free from the net as the cripple picked up the wrench and struck. Then the seal's shout of defiance and rage died in a gurgling scream, as it plummeted into the water.

Without so much as a second glance, the two men hauled in the rest of the net, threw the engine into gear, and left the cove. In the event, there was still quite a number of fish untouched, and still held in the net, so one of the men fell to cleaning and sorting the catch, while the other headed back to harbor.

The killing of the seal had been an unlawful act, as gray seals were protected between September and December each year. This the men well knew, but if anything it merely added a certain relish to the deed, being a gesture of defiance toward hated authority. They knew nothing about conservation, and would have cared little had they been told. In their view seals were vermin, and it would be better if they were all destroyed. In the public house that night, as the beer loosened their tongues, they grew more voluble in their complaints against the seals, being careful to say nothing of the murder.

For centuries mankind had hunted seals, at first for the valuable oil and hides, then later because of their habit of robbing nets and long lines. Salmon fishermen in particular hated the seals, especially the netsmen who worked in the estuaries, trapping the salmon as they entered the rivers on their return from the sea.

At times mankind took more fish from the sea than he could possibly eat. Whole catches of herring or pilchard were dumped back into the sea, because the factories were too glutted to cope with the supply. Fish were turned into food for cattle and poultry, or converted into garden fertilizers. Still trawlermen risked their lives to bring back more fish, which was often sold so cheaply that it hardly paid for the wages of the crew. Still certain individuals suffered financial loss because of the depredations of seals, and since society was not yet prepared to give any sort of compensation to those who were deprived of a living, those individuals exacted their own revenge on the seals. In spite of a plethora of fishes, man begrudged the seals their share.

By the beginning of the century, the gray seal population

had dwindled alarmingly, and since the period of greatest mortality was the time when the seals were calving, an act of parliament forbade the killing of seals during this time, at first for six weeks, and later for four months of the year. This had the desired effect, and over the years the gray seal grew in numbers, until once again the complaints of fishermen who had been robbed by seals began to make themselves heard.

Now a fresh problem arose which began to give the authorities some cause for alarm. The gray seals, like all animals, acted as hosts to parasites. One of these was the cod-worm, a nematode which in its adult, reproductive stage lived in the stomach of the seal. The droppings of the seals contained the eggs of the worm, and when the eggs hatched out the larvae swam among the plankton, to establish themselves in the small, shrimplike crustacea. These in turn were devoured by fish, and the larval worms would then embed themselves in the muscle walls of the fish.

In due course the fish would be eaten by the seals and the worms would become adult, to start the cycle all over again. They caused little harm to their hosts, but when fish were caught and sold that were infected by the worms, housewives were apt to complain. It proved useless to tell them that the worms were harmless when cooked.

Fish caught close inshore proved to be most heavily infested with worms, and a higher incidence was recorded in those areas where seals were plentiful. It seemed fairly certain that seals were the principal vectors of the parasite, and at the same time the most easily controlled hosts. Certainly the increase in seal populations coincided with the rise in incidence of the codworm, although it is still possible that other factors have caused the increase. During the past century there has been a dramatic decrease in the number of whales, together with an increase in the numbers of gulls, as well as a rise in all forms of pollution.

To appease those factions who claimed they had grounds for

complaint, a series of culls were arranged in those areas where it was claimed the seals were most numerous, and therefore causing most harm. From time to time cows and their calves were slaughtered, either by government officials, or individuals working under license. In an effort to placate those who objected to the culls, it was stated that where seals were overcrowded the calves tended to suffer, either from starvation or disease. No mention was made of the suffering of those cows bereaved of their young.

No such official cull was planned for the seals of Ramsey Sound, but in the public house that night, as the beer flowed and discussion centered around the behavior of seals, as stories were told of acts of robbery and vandalism that had occurred in the past, the two brothers, egged on by the sympathy and comments of the others in the bar, decided on a secret plan of campaign.

Late that night, after the inn had closed and the local policeman had seen that everyone present had departed in the direction of home, the two brothers gave voice to their plan. By the time they reached their farm the cold night air and the gusting wind had cleared their heads and steadied their lurching gait, but it had done nothing to appease their rancor. Still the younger of the two had his doubts.

"It's all very fine, but what good will I be on such a scheme? With this damn stick for a leg I can't even stand up on loose stones, let alone jump about."

They were sitting in the kitchen as he spoke, having a last drink and a smoke before going to bed. The other man leaned forward, patting his brother on his sound leg and grinning through a cloud of blue smoke. "Don't worry," he insisted. "The way I see it, it's better that one of us stays in the boat. We'll leave at dawn, sail quietly up to that beach on the island where the calves lie, and shoot as many of the big ones as we can before they take off into the sea. You stay in the boat, holding her just offshore, and I'll knock the youngsters on the head. Then we'll be back in time for breakfast, and there'll be a few less of the blasted things to rob our nets."

The younger man stood up, stretching, and threw his cigarette end into the fire. "Well," he yawned, "we'll see what the weather's like in the morning. I have an idea it's going to blow the slates off, and we won't be going anywhere."

As things turned out, he was quite correct in his forecast. During the night the wind backed southerly and increased in force, so that by morning low scudding clouds sent cascades of rain sweeping over the flat and featureless land, while out in the sound the white storm caps showed above the grayness of the sea, as the waves pounded and crashed on the rocks at the base of the cliffs.

Lugo lay on the beach where years ago Halic had been born. For two days now she had lain there, disinclined to feed or take exercise. She felt listless and heavy, and so she took no notice of the battle that had raged above the storm that afternoon. The challenger bull had fought gamely, but he was younger and lighter than the beachmaster and soon retired, winded, and bleeding from numerous bites. Perhaps Lugo had forgotten Halic. Certainly she did not recognize him as he swam away, defeated.

As evening wore on the storm began to abate, and as the wind dropped faint stars began to glow behind a thin curtain of cloud. Lugo was growing restless. She moved her position from time to time, rolling from one side to the other and moaning softly, partly from fear, and partly from the pain of the cramps that racked her body.

The night wore on and the stars shone more brightly as the clouds cleared. The intervals between Lugo's pains grew shorter now, and from time to time she panted, then held her breath as another spasm gripped her. In the dark hour before dawn her calf arrived, a bull calf, small but well formed, the son of Halic.

22. The Storm

Dawn broke clear and fine, each detail of twig and leaf and rock etched acid sharp on the still, crystal air. Out in the Sound the seas still ran high, the waves broken and ragged, disturbing the even swell of the Atlantic, so that the open boat pitched and heaved, riding the crest of one wave, only to fall forward and land with a timber-jarring crash in the trough of the next.

The men were tense and uneasy, partly from fear of being caught, although the chance of this was extremely remote, but mainly because of the weather. They knew the signs too well to expect it to remain fine for long. Dawn had been too bright and clear. Already dark clouds massed ominously on the southern horizon, and the wind was rising, lashing the wave caps to white foam. Now spray began to fly over the boat, drenching them and adding to their discomfort.

Even with the engine at full throttle the boat seemed to make little headway against wind and tide, but at long last the beach was in sight, with seven cows, five of them with calves, crowded on to the narrow strip of stones. They watched curiously as the men throttled down and swung the boat broadside on to the shore.

The beachmaster died first, his face blown away as a charge of shot ripped into his brain. Three of the cows were hit as they stampeded clumsily down the beach into the sea. Two died instantly, and the third swam feebly away, her movements growing slower as her life ebbed, until at last she sank below the waves. Before the men could reload, the other cows had gained the safety of the sea, but one more died as her head showed briefly above the water. Lugo escaped, leaving her calf bleating helplessly below the high wall of the cliff.

Now the boat lurched and wallowed as the storm waves crashed on the beach. Above the roaring of the sea and the whistle of the wind the cripple shouted a warning to his brother. "Don't try to land. It's too dangerous, and the calves will die anyway. Let's get away out of it."

In answer the brother picked up a pickax handle and jumped over the gunwale, landing up to his waist in the sea. Carefully he waded ashore, his feet slipping and sliding as he struggled over the loose wet stones. The first calf lay just at the edge of the tide, and he killed it with two blows of the pickax as it lay staring up at him. He was about to make his way up the steeply shelving beach when he heard his brother shout.

One of the calves was inching its way through the boulders at the end of the beach, struggling to gain the safety of the sea. With a shout the man charged across, his club raised high above his head. As he leapt across the weed-covered rock the calf suddenly spun round to face him, snarling and snapping at his foot. For a brief moment the man swayed wildly, struggling to keep his balance on the slimy treacherous rock. Then he fell heavily, to scream out loud as his thigh splintered beneath his weight.

For a long time, it seemed, he lay there, while the pain swept like fire through his body. Dimly, he was aware of his brother shouting, disconnected words heard faintly above the roar of the sea. "Going for help. . . . Can't land. . . . Tide ebbing. You'll be O.K."

He was aware only of an intense rage and hatred, white anger at the thought of his own helplessness, and hatred of his brother, who was abandoning him to his fate. Most of all he hated the seals, whose presence were the cause of his predicament. His last thought, as he drifted into unconsciousness, was regret that he had not got the calf.

The sky was dark now, and the leaping clouds brought gusts of heavy rain. Waves were breaking over the stern of the little boat, as the following wind drove it against the tide. The cripple, with engine at full throttle, fought to keep enough speed up to prevent the boat's being swamped. He ought to try and gain the shelter of the landward cliffs, but that meant a detour that would take him more than an hour, and he did not want to run the risk of shipping a wave over the side. The engine raced as the stern lifted out of the waves, then died to a growl as the boat surged forward again.

The floorboards were awash. He ought to bail, but he dared not for a moment let go of the tiller. He was coming to the chain of rocks known as the Bitches, and now the sea eddied and boiled, making the boat fight and rear like an angry beast. He crouched low in the stern, lurching as the boat threw him from side to side, cursing the sea and the black clouds, and his artificial limb that was so useless when it came to keeping his balance in a pitching boat. The engine coughed and faltered, and as fear gripped him in a tight knot, it died away altogether.

"The fuel! The reserve tank! The tap!" His lips framed the thoughts as his numbed brain grasped the situation, and he dropped the tiller and scrambled forward to the engine hatch. The tap to the reserve tank was corroded and stiff from lack of use, and as he forced it over the soft gunmetal snapped in his fingers. The tide took the boat and spun it round, lifting it high into the air before it sank stern first into the sea.

The artificial leg was hollow, and it buoyed him up, forcing his head under so that he floated upside down. For a long time he struggled with the harness that kept the leg attached, but at last the salt water entered his lungs, and he struggled no more. From time to time his foot showed above the waves, the sole

of his boot exposed to the sky. It marked his slow journey, as the tide carried him south, out of the Sound.

The tide did not ebb far. Held in check by the force of the wind it soon ceased to fall, and began to creep stealthily back over the stones. Pain roused the man on the beach as the swirling tide gently lifted his injured leg, only to drop it with a jarring crash on the rocks. Grimly, feverishly, he struggled to raise himself higher up the beach, dragging himself along on his elbows, and pushing with his good leg.

Each movement sent a fresh wave of pain surging up his body. Twice he passed out again, recovering as the relentless, questing tide plucked at his heels. Once he slid down the loose, slippery stones, and lay sobbing and cursing as the waves crashed over him. At last, delirious with pain, he lay among the tangled driftwood below the cliff, where the calves lay wide-eyed, watching him as he moaned and babbled, his fingers clutching and grasping at the stones.

Still the tide rose, and the spars and planks of wood that lay all round him began to shift and stir, creaking as the tide began to lift them. Now the waves broke over him as he huddled against the cliff. He lay watching them as they formed far out in the gray water. He saw the dark line loom closer as the sea hunched its shoulders before its spring. He saw the wave grow, to swell and tower above him, baring white fangs as it hovered for a brief moment before striking in for the kill.

With one last, desperate effort he stood up, bracing himself against the cliff as the tide sucked and pulled at the stones around his one good foot. Then, wearily, he slithered down into a squatting position, and his head drooped forward, to be slammed back against the rock as a breaking wave caught him under the chin. Methodically, the sea battered him to death against the rocks, until at last his body straightened and was pulled away on the undertow of the waves.

Out in the darkening sea Lugo waited for her calf to join her. The three calves struggled feebly among the bruising, grinding driftwood, as each time they tried to gain the safety of the open sea the waves flung them back. Now a wave higher than the rest swept diagonally along the cliff, picking up driftwood and calves and carrying them along on its crest. One calf was carried out to sea, but Lugo's son was slammed violently into a crevice among the rocks, and there his life ended, buried beneath tons of seawater and broken wood. Here too the other calf died, thrown twenty feet into the air by the breaking wave, and crushed to pulp as it fell back on to the rocks below.

Dawn came. Halic ranged through the broken waves north of the Sound, his mood as grim and relentless as the sea around him. On a small beach at the northeast tip of the island two cows lay with their calves. Purposefully, Halic swam toward them.

A warning bellow from the master bull told him he had been spotted, but he merely quickened his speed, narrowing the gap between him and his rival. The beachmaster waited just off shore, his doglike head drawn back into the folds of skin that wrinkled his massive neck. He was a very dark bull, and his bared fangs were yellow and curved. Now he surged forward to meet Halic, rearing out of the water to strike down on him.

Quickly, Halic sideslipped, and as the master bull crashed down into the sea Halic struck him hard, just below his heart. The force of the blow drove the beachmaster below the waves, but next moment he had surfaced, returning to the attack. The two seals reared out of the water, their teeth rattling like sabers as they clashed together. Halic fell back, and as the beachmaster thrust after him Halic seized him by the fore flipper, feeling the bones crack between his jaws.

Now the beachmaster had Halic by the neck, and was shaking him, thrusting him down so that his head was beneath the waves. Halic released his hold on the flipper and rolled, tearing himself free, only to turn and come rearing out of the water, shaking his head and roaring his anger as he plunged once more into the fray.

Both seals were bleeding freely now, and the foaming sea around was tinged with pink. In weight and size they were evenly matched, but Halic was the swifter of the two. Now he caught the beachmaster at the side of the throat, and they rolled over and over in the waves before sinking below the surface of the sea. For long minutes they were lost to view, and then the waters erupted in a fountain of spray as the seals exploded into the air, each still roaring defiance.

Slowly, but surely, the beachmaster was weakening. He was bleeding from a score of bites, and his injured flipper was swollen and useless. His movements grew slower, his lunges less powerful. Halic pressed home his attack, striking the beachmaster again and again with punishing blows to the heart and ribs. They were in shallow water now, close to the beach, and the force of Halic's blows sent the beachmaster crashing against the stones.

Grimly, the beachmaster made one last supreme effort, flinging himself with all his force at Halic's throat. Halic reared up, and the beachmaster's teeth met in the skin of his chest. Halic struck down, and his teeth laid the beachmaster's skull open to the bone, damaging one eye and splitting his cheek.

It was the end. The beachmaster tore free, and Halic, too weary to follow, watched him as he made off through the waves. Then Halic hauled out on to the beach and collapsed, to sleep off his exertions. When he awoke the sun was setting, and he lay at rest, his sleek, muscular body scarred with the stripes of battle, looking out over the Sound, east toward the mainland, where the brooding hills of Wales lay as though stained with blood.

A little distance away the two cows lay on the stones, accepting the presence of their new master with wary calm. The younger of the two fed her calf, lightly flippering the baby as it drew on the rich yellow milk. The older cow watched her youngster as it lay sleeping at the foot of the cliff, its rotund body twitching as an occasional fly alighted on its fur. It was now almost weaned, and lay unattended for long periods.

Night came, and with the rising tide the seals moved farther up the beach. At intervals the sobbing clamor of their voices echoed through the darkness, rising above the slap of the waves and the rattling clatter of the stones. Dawn broke crisp and fine, and with the first light the older cow lurched down the steep beach, spraying small stones to right and left as she made for the sea.

Halic followed her, swimming close behind, his lithe body emulating her every movement through the sea. As he drew alongside she snarled and snapped at him, but her teeth closed on empty air as he sideslipped and passed underneath her, his body brushing hers in a long caress.

As the sun rose, so the tempo of their courtship grew in speed and fire, and as Halic grew more insistent, more demanding, heeding less and less her halfhearted attempts to repulse him, so her resistance weakened. At last she lay, languorous and quiescent in the waves, as Halic's teeth closed over the skin of her neck and his body drew closer, to begin the long, slow mating that was the consummation of their desires. Long afterward, they slept, still locked together, until the lapping waves drew them gently apart.

Halic woke just in time to spot the doglike head of a young bull seal trying to pass between him and the beach. With a roar and a surge of white spray Halic launched himself at the intruder, who, realizing he was outmatched, turned to flee. The young seal gained the open water, but not before Halic's teeth had drawn blood from a long, shallow wound in his neck.

Now roused by the lust of battle, Halic, dominant and refreshed, returned to his love of the morning and possessed her with a savagery that quickly left them spent and exhausted. The cow returned to the beach, but Halic lingered on in the shallow sea, cruising slowly back and forth along the tiny strip of beach.

He had reached maturity, and here on this island sanctuary, in company with the seabirds and the rolling, restless tides, Halic, wise in the ways of the sea, would spend the rest of his life. Yet how long he lived depended on man-made laws difficult to enforce, and subject to variation at his whim.

The land was old, older than the bronze men, whose ghosts still haunted the somber valleys and hills. It was old when the ice came, and the glaciers carved their writings on the face of long lost regions where the tide now ebbed and flowed. Yet the sea was older than the land.

Between Halic and the mainland lay the Sound, a wide and turbulent expanse of water where the tide raced to and fro, and the whistling wind, cold and clean, ripped the white caps from the waves, to hurl them against the jagged rocks. Beyond the Sound the flower-strewn cliffs dropped sheer to the sea a hundred feet below, forming a formidable barrier to what was, for man, a wild and inhospitable place. This was the Sound of the seals.

Yet the gulf which separated Halic from the world of man was infinitely wider and deeper than the Sound, and the barriers of ignorance and prejudice were higher and stonier than the cliffs. The seals had renounced any claim they might have had on the land, and asked only to be left in peace. They are uncommunicative, and their minds remain as difficult to fathom as the deep waters that lie beyond the Continental shelf.

Halic might well live on for another two decades. His future, like that of the whales and the turtles, the seabirds and the salmon, lies in our hands. Perhaps one day mankind will cross the Sound, to learn what perhaps the seals have understood all along, that life can only be sacred, may only be permitted to survive, for just as long as it is prepared to support and serve other forms of life. Beyond that there can be no understanding, no beauty, and no hope.